Caroline Rudd
Sport Science

KU-329-435

# PATHWAYS TO EXCELLENCE

The British Institute of Sports Coaches
1992
Annual Conference

Editor: Rosita Whittall

4-6 December 1992
The Hilton National Hotel
East Midlands Airport

PATHWAYS TO EXCELLENCE

The proceedings of the 1992 BISC Annual Conference.

Copyright © 1993 The National Coaching Foundation.

ISBN 0-947850-97-X

First published 1993 by The National Coaching Foundation, 114 Cardigan Road, Headingley, Leeds LS6 3BJ.

Printed and bound in Great Britain.

This book is copyright under the Berne Convention. All rights are reserved. Apart from any fair dealing for the purpose of private study, research, criticism, or review, as permitted under the Copyright, Designs and Patents Act, 1988, no part of this publication may be reproduced, stored in a retrieval system or transmitted in any form or by any means, electronic, electrical, chemical, mechanical, optical, photocopying, recording or otherwise, without the prior written permission of the copyright owner. Enquiries should be addressed to the National Coaching Foundation.

### Editor's Note

Some of the papers in this publication were transcribed and edited from verbal presentations given at the Conference, and it is hoped that the edited versions do justice to the quality of the original presentations.

### Acknowledgements

The National Coaching Foundation wishes to acknowledge the generous support of The Sports Council and the Save & Prosper Group Ltd.

# Contents

# Preface

*What an inspiration! The Conference presented me with a tremendous opportunity to gain an abundance of knowledge, and from the stimulating environment created I was able to draw upon and benefit from the wealth of talent and experience present.*

This was the reaction of one football coach from Wales following the fourth international congress on the theme of *'The Growing Child in Competitive Sport'* organised by The British Institute of Sports Coaches under the title *'Pathways to Excellence'*.

The Conference was aimed at teachers, coaches, parents, and administrators from clubs and governing bodies of sport who are concerned with the development of the whole child in the pursuit of sporting excellence, to ensure that the process of nurturing talent is achieved in a safe and positive way.

The participation of growing children in competitive sport is a subject which can arouse passion and controversy, enthusiasm and cynicism in equal measure. Many youngsters seek to emulate their sporting heroes, often aided and abetted by supportive parents whose hopes and aspirations for their offspring can sometimes be over-ambitious or premature. Many sports organisations are also keen to identify talent at an early age, and enrol youngsters on progressive development programmes of intensive training and competition.

People love champions, but producing them needs considerable expertise and careful planning if the best interests of the whole child are to be protected. It is important to ensure that early sporting experiences are purposeful, positive and enjoyable and lay good foundations for a healthy life in later years, as well as encouraging young performers to achieve their potential. There can be many pitfalls along the way and failure to recognise and avoid them not only represents missed opportunities in terms of maximising talent, but also can have detrimental effects on the overall development of the growing child.

Raising awareness of problem areas and creating suitable programmes for young people is the proper concern of all who are involved in competitive sport. *'Pathways to Excellence'* closely examines the progression of young performers from foundation activities through participation and competition in the search for sporting excellence and presents practical guidance for coaches, teachers, parents and administrators on ways to ensure sound development commensurate with the growth stage and ability of the child.

Questions raised and answered at the Conference will have great significance not only for the future of sport, but also for the well-being of future generations in terms of their long term enjoyment of an active and healthy lifestyle.

The Conference was attended by 180 delegates including representatives from Australia, Canada, Hungary, Kuwait, Poland, United Kingdom, and the USA.

**Geoff Cooke OBE**
**Chief Executive, The British Institute of Sports Coaches.**

# I Want my Coach to be... The View of a Young Athlete

## Neil Armstrong

*Dr Neil Armstrong is Director of the Physical Education Association Research Centre, University of Exeter. He is President of the Physical Education Association of Great Britain and Northern Ireland and a former Chairman of the British Association of Sports Sciences. Neil's academic interests are in the field of Paediatric Exercise Science, and he is currently directing a longitudinal study of children's fitness, health and well-being.*

I want my coach to be a person who cares about my development and understands that I am not a mini-adult. For the purpose of this talk I will concentrate upon some physiological issues, but I also expect my coach to understand the psychological, mechanical and social issues involved in coaching me.

In order to contract, my muscles require energy and I obtain this energy from the breakdown of adenosine triphosphate (ATP) which is stored in my muscles. Unfortunately, like adults, I am able only to store small amounts of ATP, perhaps sufficient for about one to two seconds of maximal running. ATP must therefore be regenerated very quickly to allow me to continue exercising. Initially ATP is re-synthesised from the breakdown of another high energy substance, creatine phosphate (CP), which is also stored in my muscles. However, my muscular stores of CP are also limited and are only able to support maximal exercise for a further four to five seconds. Nevertheless, my muscular concentration of high energy phosphates (ATP and CP) is very similar to that of an adult and I use them up at much the same rate as an adult during intensive exercise. I am, therefore, as well equipped as an adult to compete in activities of maximal intensity but very short duration (eg. sprinting).

Well before my high energy phosphates are used up, more ATP will be provided from the breakdown of carbohydrate (stored as glycogen in the muscles and liver) to pyruvic acid. Unfortunately, in the early stages of exercise when oxygen consumption is low, and during very intensive exercise when pyruvic acid production exceeds the capacity of the aerobic system to oxidise it, a build up of pyruvic acid results in the formation of lactic acid. Lactic acid accumulates in my muscles and will eventually bring muscular contraction to a halt. This anaerobic energy system is often called lactacid energy system. My ability to generate energy through this system will improve as I get older and more mature. At the moment I have a severe functional disadvantage compared with an adult when performing strenuous activities of between 10 and 60 seconds duration.

The oxygen transport (or aerobic) system is relatively slow to adapt to the demands of exercise, and the rate at which ATP can be generated anaerobically greatly exceeds that of the aerobic system. The aerobic system is, however, the most efficient in terms of ATP production and because of its ability to use fat, in the form of fatty acids, as an energy source it has a much greater capacity for energy generation than the anaerobic systems. During prolonged exercise my performance therefore depends largely upon my ability to deliver oxygen to my muscles. The maximum energy output of my aerobic system is best described by my maximal oxygen uptake ($VO_2$ max) which is widely recognised as the best single measure of my cardiopulmonary fitness. My $VO_2$ max will increase with age, and at first glance I appear to be placed at a disadvantage in comparison with an adult. However, my body mass is much smaller and my mass-related $VO_2$ max is at least as good as an adult's, so in tasks which involve moving my body mass I will not be disadvantaged. My sister is less fortunate in this context because a greater proportion of her increase in body mass with maturity will be fat. Also, she will not experience the same increase in haemoglobin concentration as I will.

Although I am generally well-equipped to exercise aerobically during very prolonged exercise (eg. long distance running) I will be at a disadvantage when compared to an adult. This is because my movements are less efficient, I have lower reserves of power and smaller stores of muscle glycogen. When entering me for long distance events I want my coach to consider the surface I will run on in relation to my immature skeleton. Furthermore, the environmental conditions are important as my temperature regulating system is not fully developed and my ability to sweat is limited. I have a large body surface area in relation to my muscle mass which means that I am vulnerable at extremes of temperature.

I want my coach to stress the importance of taking sensible precautions before, during, and after training sessions. I want him/her to consider appropriate footwear and dress in relation to the weather conditions and my current health. I should not be allowed to train if I am suffering from a viral illness. I want to be taught how to warm-up correctly before exercising and how to progressively cool-down following the session so that I can gradually assume responsibility for my own warm-up and cool-down.

Due to possible damage which may occur to the growth zones of my skeleton, I want my coach to be cautious about maximal resistance training (eg. using weights) until my growth spurt is virtually over. On the other hand, the capillary blood supply to my muscles is highly responsive during the growth period and local muscular endurance exercises are particularly suitable. My younger siblings (pre-pubescent) should be encouraged to use sub maximal resistance, perhaps using their own body weight (eg. press-ups, pull-ups) but a balanced programme of heavier weight training will be advantageous to me as I move into late adolescence.

Poor flexibility can be a cause of overuse injuries, and imbalance between muscle strength and flexibility may result in muscle or joint injury. I want my coach to teach me how to carry out a programme of flexibility (stretching) exercises which will not cause damage to my joints or vertebral column. I would prefer to use static stretching, as there is much less chance of tearing the soft tissue and less likelihood of causing muscular soreness. I am willing to progress into the use of more advanced techniques (eg. assisted passive stretching, proprioceptive neuromuscular facilitation) but I must be in control of assisted stretching of my body.

I want my coach to understand fully the principles of training – overload, progression, specificity, reversibility, adaptability, evaluation and periodisation – but I want my training prescription explained to me in terms I can understand, such as in the FIT system (ie. Frequency – how often?; Intensity – how hard?; Time – how long?). Appropriate training prescriptions for me, using the FIT system, are available elsewhere (Armstrong, 1992).

The effects of appropriate training programmes on my energy systems will be similar to those expected in adults, but lactacid training will probably be of little value to me until I reach late adolescence. Lactacid anaerobic training is very strenuous and I want my coach to plan carefully when to include it in my training cycle. Heavy anaerobic training will probably require an increase in the carbohydrate content of my diet.

I want my coach to be aware of the sports science support programme available in the United Kingdom and to use the laboratories accredited by the British Association of Sports Sciences (details available from the National Coaching Foundation) to indicate my strengths and weaknesses and to enable optimum training regimes to be designed and monitored. It is, however, often difficult to simulate sports performance in a laboratory and my coach must realise that the value of non-sport-specific tests decreases as the more patterns tested become more removed from the actual performance. Similarly, I may find the equipment a problem as apparatus designed for use with adults may not be appropriate for me. Nevertheless, laboratory assessment of my performance is likely to be of more value than use of field tests (see Armstrong, 1990).

I want to fulfil my potential, so I need my coach to be aware of the latest developments in sports science such as lactate training (see *Coaching Focus*, No 21, 1992) but also to be aware of the limitations of using adult training programmes with me. For example, the recommended training intensity for adults has often been set at a blood lactate level of 4mM, but training set at this lower level is likely to be too intense for me. I have much lower blood lactate levels during exercise than an adult and it has been suggested that a lactate training level of 2.5mM would be a more appropriate intensity (see Armstrong and Welsman, 1993 for details).

In conclusion, I want my coach to understand that I am adequately equipped to handle activities which require short but intensive exercise or more prolonged periods of moderate exercise. I am not well-equipped to cope with training which demands a significant contribution from the lactacid system. I will be responsive to muscular endurance training, but work with heavy weights should probably be avoided until I am in late adolescence. Training regimes introduced at the appropriate time in my development will induce changes of a similar magnitude to those expected in adults. A period of detraining will cause many of these changes to gradually decay. There is no strong evidence to support the suggestion that training must be started early in order to experience success as an adult and encouraging me to specialise at a young age may be counter-productive. I want my coach to be sensitive to the fact that childhood success in sport is often linked to rate of maturation – early maturing boys have a distinct advantage in most sports but with girls it is often the late maturers who are successful (eg. gymnasts). I want to be encouraged to internalise the motivation to exercise so that when the extrinsic motivation of the coach is removed I will carry on exercising throughout my adult life.

If I am helped to understand the principles underlying fitness and health, and taught how to develop my own training programme which can periodically be re-appraised and modified as I grow older and my aspirations change, I will always be grateful to my coach.

## References

Armstrong, N (1990) **Field testing children's physical fitness.**
Sportcoach. 5-6, October

Armstrong, N (1992) **Children and exercise II – training responses.**
Athletics Coach. 26, 5-9

Armstrong, N and Welsman, J (1993) **Training programmes for young athletes.**
In MJ Lee (ed) The Development of Coaching Programmes for Children, London,
E & F Spon (in press).

# Laying Good Foundations

## Rick Bailey

*Rick Bailey is the Head of Sports Development in the Department of Recreation and Community Services of Birmingham City Council. He is an active member of the current England Swimming team management, and also Honorary Secretary to the Great Britain Swimming Technical Committee and the ASA Swimming Committee.*

My presentation will be in four parts:

- Our rationale/strategy behind the work with young children of primary school age.
- Sports Development and work with primary school education in Birmingham.
- Difficulties of implementation.
- What is needed in the future.

### Rationale/Strategy Behind the Work

A review of population figures for the City of Birmingham pre-1991 census will demonstrate that the increasing birth rate in the mid to late 1980s is now increasing numbers in the primary school phase of education, and those increased numbers are expected to continue to rise into the mid-1990s.

This, for us, will be justification enough to pay greater attention to the needs of young people (7-11 years) through our work in Sports Development and the need to introduce schemes and programmes to cater for this increasing school population.

In our strategy document – *'Sports Development in Birmingham, Strategy for the 1990s'* we recognise that young people, particularly those of primary school age, are a key target group within our overall strategy for sport in Birmingham. Increasing numbers will, we believe, place an increasing emphasis on the need and demand for teaching, coaching and instructional opportunities within this area of the population. There is some evidence to show, which we expect to be borne out in statistics from the recent census, that the birth rate amongst the ethnic population in Birmingham is growing at a faster rate than that of the indigenous white/European population. We recognise that our traditional approach to sport needs to be modified and sympathetic to the needs of that increasing element of the school population. The phrase 'Catch 'em young' is expressed at many levels of sport and it is usually followed by the remark, 'If we don't, somebody else will!' I believe that such policies contribute greatly to the loss and natural wastage of an undeniably large pool of talented young sports people long before they can ever aspire to achieving their ambition and dreams in sport.

Many sports seek to influence choice and opportunity by modifying the rules and structures of the senior game/activity to create opportunities for children at primary school age. Many, however, particularly individual sports, challenge young children at far too early a stage in their development to participate and even compete, in an 'adult' version. This, I believe, places too much emphasis on the activity and less on the overall development of the child at this crucial age.

In my own sport of swimming, guilty for too long of exposing young people to competitive influences at too early an age, the Technical Swimming Committee is putting forward to next year's Council meeting of the Amateur Swimming Association a proposal to change ASA law which will effectively mean that the Club, and the coach, will create opportunity and nurture the young performer through the early stages of the development process. The opportunity to participate in individual events of an 'open' nature will not be available until the age of 11 at Regional level and 12 at National level.

A more basic issue for Sports Development teams is the recognition that Local Authorities, despite the pressures of Government legislation, have at last come to terms with the fact that the provision of public facilities for sport and recreation are there for the communities who wish to use them. Opportunities at all levels of the Sports Development 'Continuum' need to be developed to maximise their use. It is at this point that I introduce my first reference to the word **partnership** and demonstrate those factors which I believe influence foundation or 'grass roots' sports.

### Sports Development and Primary School Education in Birmingham

If I was totally honest I would say at this point, 'Why are you asking me about sports development work in the area of primary school education?' I don't believe that I can demonstrate a highly successful blueprint for the implementation of this work in Birmingham. Perhaps that's the message, and what I should be conveying to you is that there is a tremendous amount of work to be done in this area of sports development. For this reason, I would commend to you the case study presentation by Jeremy Woodhouse on the Dudley project because, I believe, embodied within the objectives being tested in consultation and conjunction with primary schools in the Dudley area, this will be a model of success which we all can inherit for our mutual benefit.

I believe we have identified a way forward for our work in Birmingham. The work of the Curriculum Support Service in Physical Education is a progressive and effective one for the teachers in our City schools. Sports Development recognises the importance of partnership with our colleagues in the CSS team where, by offering support and expertise in key areas of our work, we can support them to deliver the curriculum.

The creation of the Physical Education National Curriculum is, for me, a major step forward in the development of PE in schools, and ultimately the development of sport for the young. It has acted as a catalyst to stimulate the minds of educationalists, sports coaches and administrators alike. It has provided a framework in which teachers are encouraged to deliver and we, for our part, can be recognised for the support that we can offer in that delivery.

Local management of schools has clearly had an impact on the delivery of sport/ physical education in schools and nowhere has this been more evident than at primary school level. The number of direct requests received by Sports Development Officers from primary school Headteachers is evidence enough to show that there is an urgent need to interpret the partnership in a positive way for the benefit of young children.

Our reaction must be either a supported or a co-ordinated response through, and by, Curriculum Support Services. In this way our work in Sports Development bears the CSS 'kite-mark' of approval. Our development work in football, cricket and gymnastics bears testimony to this association. Similarly in swimming our own City Award Scheme, based on watermanship skills as opposed to distance based badges, illustrates a co-ordinated approach with teachers to swimming activities throughout the City.

My most immediate concern is that neither we, nor the Education Service, have the resources to meet the demand from schools in their search for support and help in delivering Key Stages One and Two of the Physical Education National Curriculum. As a consequence many schools are turning to the independent sports 'Consultant' who sees coaching opportunities with young children both inside and outside the curriculum as a golden opportunity to make money. Some such initiatives, often associated with the appearance of a star or personality in that sport, frequently demonstrate the unacceptable face of sport in the educational process of the child. I see this as an issue for the national governing bodies of sport as they seek to initiate development plans. The introduction of regional and local development officers, who have an objective to reach the schools and school children, must be carefully monitored and directed by us through existing channels of communication.

We have been delighted to welcome recently four Regional Development Officers into our area and provide them with an office base. In this way we are beginning to open up our links and pathways for those charged with the development of sport, not only in Birmingham, but in the West Midland region. Other examples of our work in conjunction with primary schools include:

- the development of extra curricular activity on school sites – Little Leagues
- the organisation and co-ordination of primary school festivals of sport for local schools in the area – Primary Schools Hockey Festival
- support from primary school associations, eg. Birmingham Primary Schools FA, Schools Gymnastics
- INSET courses for teachers.

Other initiatives in which we are involved as a Sports Development Team can also contribute towards this important work with primary schools. Our Community Sports Club, an initiative in partnership with the local Sports Advisory Council and the Regional Sports Council, is initially aimed at identifying a role for sports clubs and how they can contribute towards junior development in our leisure centres and sports facilities. Ultimately this project is aimed at strengthening the club structure in Birmingham. But I also believe there is a parallel exercise to be undertaken in the development of pathways and exit routes through the various stages of Sports Development to complete the link between clubs and schools.

We are very fortunate to have been selected as a Champion Coaching City. I believe Katie Donovan and her colleagues initially felt that Birmingham was too big to implement such a scheme at local level. We hope to prove her wrong, but in referring to the Champion Coaching Project we firmly believe that our work with younger people of primary school age is going to be important to us in developing the foundations and pathways into this project.

## Difficulties of Implementation

I would like to examine for a moment the relationship which exists between Sports Development and Education, and in particular, the interface between sport and physical education.

Sport is perceived as being performance orientated whereas physical education is more process orientated and as a direct result of the planning, performing and evaluating activity.

Sport, whether it be individual or team orientated, places emphasis on the activity and tends to ignore any lateral influences it may have on other associated or totally different sports activities. However, through physical education the emphasis is clearly on the overall development of the child. This is invariably long term and very much a broad based curriculum when relating to primary school age children.

I see sport in the context of school physical education as being part of a total school culture whereas sport in a wider sense exists and operates within its own environment and has its own specific culture.

If we look at a typical primary school teacher we see that first and foremost they are 'generalist' in what they deliver to the school pupils. They do have, within that broad generalist framework, a responsibility to deliver physical education to their class. As a consequence there are significant implications for physical education in primary schools and particularly as a direct consequence of the Physical Education National Curriculum at Key Stages One and Two.

It is not unusual to find that initial teacher training for a Bachelor of Education Degree demonstrates an average of 20 to 60 hours over the four year period of training devoted to physical education. Within a Post graduate Certificate of Education course the average can be as low as 10 to 20 hours over the one year. Even main course students in physical education spend little more than two years of their total course studying the **teaching** of physical education and the practical aspects associated with the subject. How often do we hear a reference to the fact that students of physical education are becoming increasingly less equipped to deal with the wide range of practical physical education skills and commitments?

The result of such a situation is that our primary school teacher has a great deal of knowledge about children and their overall development. They have full responsibility for the planning/teaching and assessing of children's work in all curriculum areas. As a consequence of their initial teacher training there is inevitably going to be some lack of confidence with content knowledge particularly in practical subjects like physical education and music etc. On top of that there are increasing pressures being placed on primary school teachers to meet the demands placed upon them, of new educational thinking and legislation. Finally there is a time commitment to a profession and all it entails.

## What is Needed in the Future?

I believe the answer has to be based on a theme of working together and of partnership between the various agencies; all able to demonstrate a willingness and a contribution to the development of the primary school child.

In Sports Development we see this as facilitating the opportunity for teachers to become more aware, more confident and more skilful in delivering aspects of the PE National Curriculum in their schools. Our contribution through INSET via the vehicle of the Curriculum Support Service is our priority.

We see this partnership as actively supporting the work of individual Physical Education Advisers, and we certainly see the need for essential changes in higher education to facilitate better qualified primary school teachers able to deliver the full PE National Curriculum in their schools.

For the most part we recognise that governing bodies of sport are addressing the importance of the Physical Educational National Curriculum, by working and producing Curriculum Packs to assist school teachers in specific areas of activity. From a Sports Development Officer's point of view the availability of such materials is a welcome and essential ingredient in providing advice and support to primary school teachers. However, if Sports Development is to move forward in partnership with Education, and in particular the primary education sector, we have to ask ourselves some very pertinent questions:

1 Am I the right person to work in Education? Who makes that selection and on what criteria is that selection based? What relevant training would be appropriate for Sports Development Officers to undertake or have as accredited prior learning before going into the primary sector?

2 Do I want to work in a supportive role? Do Sports Development Officers ever see themselves as supporters as opposed to initiators, and how would I respond to a situation of having to negotiate my input with the class teacher?

3 What do I have to offer primary school children and/or teachers? Does my involvement as a Coach at the Olympic Games give me the qualities and qualifications to become involved in this particular area? Should it be curricular or preferably extra curricular?

4 What are my motivations or intentions for wanting to work with primary school children? Are they seen as a development process or do we see this as a mere talent identification process?

The debate will go on; what will not change immediately is the urgent need for all agencies involved in sport to work to provide a supported and well informed resource, which will enable the school teacher to lay a solid foundation for future participation and the health of future generations.

# Equal Pathways – Genuine Commitment

## The British Sports Association for the Disabled

The title of this year's Conference is 'The Growing Child in Competitive Sport' and BISC makes no apology for focusing on the youth aspect once again.

Whilst BSAD applaud BISC's commitment to the 'growing child', we make no apology for including this Conference paper in an attempt to address what may be yet another missed opportunity in the development of sport for young people.

We are sure that some group sessions and case studies presented this weekend will show understanding, knowledge, and a commitment to the provision of sport for people with a disability. We are also sure that some of the teachers, coaches, local authority and governing body officers are equally committed to the provision of equality of sporting opportunity, but perhaps not all – perhaps not even many. In the sport and disability field, our practical experience at all levels tells us that there is still a long way to go before many people involved in sport and recreation have even a basic understanding of the abilities and needs of people with disabilities.

In this short paper we cannot hope to provide all the answers. Indeed we do not know **all** the answers – but we are certainly aware of the problems. We do not intend to question your commitment; however, the time has come to turn the words of commitment into action.

**Perhaps you would like to ask yourself the following questions:**

- Are there any children with a disability in your junior squads or sessions? If not – have you ever considered why?

- How confident do you and your colleagues feel in providing for children with a disability?

- How many coaches/teachers/administrators do you know who have a disability? If not many – why?

- How many coaching courses have you been on which include disability issues in the syllabus?

- Is your venue **fully** accessible?
  Are you sure?

- Does your school, club, department or governing body have a policy regarding people with a disability?
  If so – has it made a difference?
  Have words been turned into action?

- Have you ever consulted people with a disability in your plans and strategies?
  If so – how often and at what stages?

One other question we might ask is 'can you identify sporting talent in a disabled child?' Many of us believe in our own ability to identify sporting talent. For a coach it may mean five nights a week out on the track, observing and analysing sprinting techniques – for others it may be a regular critical appraisal of a televised football match from the comfort of their own living room. If our coach or armchair critic was confronted with disabled sports people would they continue to exercise their skills in observation and constructive criticisms, or would they simply comment on how 'marvellous' people like that are?

Some disabled sportspeople certainly are marvellous athletes – others are just average participants, the same as you and I.

## Identifying Potential Talent

In September 1992, the Great Britain Paralympic team returned from Barcelona with 40 gold, 47 silver and 41 bronze medals, finishing third overall. The games were an immense success with capacity crowds who witnessed the pinnacle of sporting competition.

The major events in the 1992 Paralympics were:

| | | | | |
|---|---|---|---|---|
| Archery | Power/Weight Lifting | Athletics | Shooting | Basketball |
| Soccer | Boccia | Swimming | Cycling | Table Tennis |
| Fencing | Volleyball | Judo | | |

Many athletes will already be preparing for the 1996 games in Atlanta.

Many potential athletes are in school now awaiting the opportunity to participate and succeed. These children, if given that opportunity, will participate, succeed and excel in the year 2000 games.

## Where are the Young Athletes?

Some are in segregated schools, others are in mainstream. There are many young people in school now who would like to participate in sport and may even be potential paralympians. We must not underestimate a child's potential.

## What's a Fast Time or a Long Throw?

In order to give young people the chance to participate and achieve, we must understand the concept of sport for people with a disability. We must understand that Claire Bishop and Peter Hull achieved gold medals and new world records for the same swimming event.

| | | | |
|---|---|---|---|
| Claire Bishop | 50M Freestyle | 32.52 | Claire (15 years old) is a below elbow amputee |
| Peter Hull | 50M Freestyle | 1.09.28 | Peter has a congenital absence of legs and short arms |

**The only difference is their disability – the similarity is the exceptional performance.**

In an attempt to ensure athletes are measured on their ability and not disability, classification systems are used; these can be complex and controversial but are necessary. At a junior level where we are looking to encourage participation and allow individuals to achieve success, it is important to have appropriate expectations.

If our expectations are realistic we can allow children to experience success whether in the Physical Education lesson, the local Leisure Centre or in the Paralympic Games. As we are now aware the National Curriculum for Physical Education entitles all children to a broad and balanced curriculum – made appropriate to each individual need.

Everyone who is involved in sports provision believes in the benefits that can be derived from all levels of participation in Physical Education and Sport, and most of us believe in the equality of opportunity.

The fact is, that to provide equality in our sports provision to young people with a disability, we must be active and we will not realise our beliefs until we do.

# Talent Identification and Development

## Dr Sue Campbell MBE

*Sue Campbell trained as a Physical Education Teacher and taught in Manchester. She spent four years as Assistant Director of Physical Education at Leicester University before taking up the post of Lecturer at Loughborough University. She then moved to the East Midlands Sports Council as Regional Officer and in 1985 was appointed Chief Executive of the National Coaching Foundation. Her sporting achievements include international athlete and netball player; senior athletics coach and team manager for England Womens Basketball.*

The search for potential champions at an early age has become an increasingly significant aspect of high performance sport in recent years and is generally considered necessary if youngsters are to succeed in a given sport. Selection procedures now attempt to predict future capacities as well as identify present performance. The old Eastern bloc countries employed such methods for many years and it is only fairly recently that we in the West have come to appreciate the potential of a well-structured talent identification and development programme.

The major difficulty we have with this type of system is the ethical one. Selection of children at an increasingly early age for involvement in high competitive sports can conjure up unacceptable images of control and exploitation. Young children are vulnerable to manipulation and, if they have been pushed into high-performance sport, they are in danger of 'burn-out' and eventually drop out from sport altogether.

In Britain we need a new approach to excellence in sport which fosters the well-being of every young person while positively supporting and encouraging individual achievement.

The last 25 years have seen an extraordinary development in the field of sport, leisure and recreation. It was only 25 years ago that the first publicly funded indoor sports facilities were built; it is only within the past 25 years that leisure and recreation departments have been created. It is only 18 years since the Sports Council was established. This growth has been welcome but it has left a range of organisations at local, regional and national level which may, in some areas, duplicate each other's activities. In other sectors reluctant or recalcitrant isolationism has meant that the best service is not being provided, clearly due to a lack of coordination and cooperation. If individuals and teams are to flourish in terms of performance and excellence, it is essential that there is a much clearer definition of responsibilities in all sectors.

Those involved in improving their performance and reaching excellence have often been classified as the 'elite'. In turn, the word 'elite' has been seen in exclusive rather than inclusive terms, with a focus on a small number of top level participants.

However, it is important to stress that performance sport exists at all levels. It includes those who want to get from the second eleven into the first; from the club tennis team into the county team; from the regional squad into the national squad and so on. It encompasses a vast number of people who simply want to improve and reach their own levels of excellence.

In relation to those who do reach publicly acclaimed levels of excellence, can they, should they, be classified as elite? The answer is yes. There should be no apology, but rather a determination to provide elite services for elite performers. This change of attitude will be essential if the good are to be allowed to become the best.

*Every young person has a right to achieve excellence but do they have that opportunity?*

This paper will be divided into three distinct sections:-

| | |
|---|---|
| What is talent? | DETECTION |
| How do we identify talent? | SELECTION |
| What is required to develop talent? | PERFECTION |

### Detection – What is Talent?

If we begin to identify those factors which make up talented performers they fall into a number of categories:

- Physique.
- Mental Attitude.
- Motor Control.
- Ability to Learn.
- Technical/Tactical/Strategical Ability.
- Flair.

The great performers make complex tasks look simple, they appear to have more time to make their decisions and they have moments when they uniquely express their skill (flair). Is this all learnt or is it all genetic? Certainly having the right parents helps.

There are several anatomical, physiological and psychological factors which contribute to the identification of potential sporting talents in children. Qualities such as flexibility, movement coordination in time and space, reaction speed, local muscular endurance and variations in tendons and ligaments are all largely genetically determined.

However, talent development also depends on competitive structures, willingness to train, recovery capacity, training facilities and effective coaching.

Perhaps the greatest area in which parents play a significant role is the psychological and emotional support they give their children. Parental encouragement and involvement can be an enormous spur to the aspiring young performer, but too much parental pressure can become an intolerable stressor.

At what age should we attempt to identify talent? In some countries, for example China, young people with talent are identified at a very early age and transferred to specialist schools. This does not fit with the philosophy of the British sporting culture. The danger is that we leave it too late or in fact have no system at all, thus leaving talented youngsters to slip through the system.

The next issue we must address is 'can we test for talent?' There are five areas in which testing does take place:

- Physical measurements.
- Motor ability.
- Psychological testing.
- Learning ability (related to sport not academic ability).
- Sports skills testing.

Before testing, it is important that some norms are established for particular activities at particular maturational stages. In the past in the USSR about 80% of the country's coaches worked with athletes between the ages of 6 and 18. Each coach was equipped with the characteristics of a prototype athlete for each sport; the kind of strength, speed, power and endurance demanded by the sport, the optimal age at which these qualities could be developed and the most effective exercises for the specific sport. Special criteria for the identification of young talented athletes include height, bone structure, muscle composition and other criteria such as the level of motor capability for physical components, the ability to learn and genetic factors.

Predicting the performance potential of young people in order to guide them to the most suitable event is a complicated task. While some help can certainly be obtained through testing, this can only provide data to inform the coach's judgement; it cannot be viewed in isolation.

### Selection – How Do We Identify Talent?

Who are these talented performers; where do they come from; do they simply emerge? Many people interested in sport have often stood on a touchline or at the side of a court, track or pool and identified that an individual had a clear talent. The frustration usually lies in knowing that the talent will not be allowed to flourish, due to a wide range of factors – no leadership, absence of facilities, no financial resources, poor availability of coaching.

So much of attaining improved performance and excellence is knowing what goal is realistic and can be achieved. That is not to deny good fortune and unexpected events, but for most individuals the key will lie in the planning process. If this is true for the individual it is applicable also at local, regional and national level for those organisations responsible for helping individuals realise their potential.

In the past decade there has been an attempt to persuade local authorities, regional sports associations and national governing bodies of sport to produce strategic documents related to providing for performance and excellence. Many have proved beneficial, most have missed the mark in that they have not provided the framework within which talent can come through.

As part of its work in promoting performance and excellence, the Sports Council has produced two sets of guidelines which contribute towards the planning process:

1  Guidelines for local agencies in performance planning.

2  Guidelines for national sports bodies in forward planning.

However, discrete planning by different agencies is not enough. There must be a corporate approach to the planning process, leading to knowledge of each other's plans and integration of those plans – all to provide a clearer pathway for the individual progressing through different stages on the performance ladder.

Performance pathways need to be clearly established for young people by integrating the work of all agencies: schools, clubs, local authorities, national governing bodies, youth service and parent teacher associations. Talent should be identified from as wide a base as possible. Too much selectivity too soon can lead to a scarcity of numbers later on and the exclusion of late developers. Performance pathways need to be carefully managed to ensure that young people are exposed to the right competition, coaching and support. An example of a performance pathway is shown below.

---

Primary School
Foundation experience – movement literacy

Secondary School
New National Curriculum provision

After school sport programmes
Coordinated by the school and/or the community

(Junior) Club sport squads

Schools/Clubs representative teams

Regional/County/District Development Squads
(age group related)

Regional/County/District Representative teams
(age group related)

National Squads
(age group related)

National Team
(age group related)

---

The people who are involved in talent identification at each stage along the performance pathway – parents, teachers, coaches, scouts – are rarely trained. We must identify the skills they need and begin to provide some systematic training for those involved in the front line of talent identification.

**Perfection – What is Required to Develop Talent?**

This section will consider two separate areas – the environment necessary to develop talent and the management of talent. A number of factors are critical in talent identification – coaching, sports science, sports medicine, facilities, time and opportunity.

One of the most important factors in the development of talent is quality of leadership provided. East Germany was often cited as the greatest 'manufacturer' of gold medal winners in the world. How did they achieve their success? Was it laboratory wizards cooking up miracle drugs that could not be detected or was it highly advanced equipment and technology? Perhaps it was both, but they also produced a large number of teachers and coaches for their massive sports programmes, which ranged from national teams to children's instructional classes in small towns. At every club or school you could find at least one coach or teacher who had spent a minimum of four years in the main College of Physical Culture in Leipzig learning about sports science, coaching/teaching methodology and training theory. East Germany had more than a quarter of a million certified coaches and 160,000 referees, umpires and judges.

In the UK, sports coaches come from a variety of backgrounds and enter sport for many different reasons – they may be ex-athletes themselves; they may wish to work with young people; or they may be interested parents of young performers. At one end of the scale, coaches can be described as an enthusiastic army of volunteers and at the other, a dedicated group of top professionals.

It is vital for the future of UK sport that we create a strong, well educated and effectively deployed coaching force in order that talent can be nurtured and developed in a systematic manner. While accepting that the bulk of coaching in the UK will always be voluntary, we need the development of a professional and semi-professional infrastructure of coaches. We need to continue moving towards the professionalisation of coaching with:

- high standards of training for all coaches
- a strong professional association to ensure that standards are maintained and that coaches work to well-designed performance and development plans
- an agreed code of ethics to ensure that all participants are protected against bad practice
- the development of employment opportunities and a career structure for coaches.

Today's sports coaches and performers require the best possible information on a range of topics including diet, fitness, training and mental preparation. Knowledge in sports science is continually increasing and we have some excellent people working in this area in the UK. There are now answers to questions like 'Can an athlete control his/her nerves before a big race?'; 'What are the best methods of analysing matches?'; 'How do you know a particular fitness training schedule is having the desired effect?'

No one would claim that they know all the answers, but much of the guesswork can be removed through discussions between coach and sports scientists. The trouble is that in the past they rarely spoke the same language. Close cooperation between science and the practical side is vital if real progress is to be made. Performers and coaches require access to appropriate sports science facilities and expertise. At present many of these resources are to be found in Institutes of Higher Education. The identification and accreditation of such expertise undertaken by the British Association of Sports Science has allowed the Governing Bodies to know where to turn for advice and guidance. Equally important has been the help given to NGBs to assist them identify their sports science requirements at all levels and to guide them in the planning of appropriate support programmes. To sum up the value of sports science to sport we can simply say 'Why guess when you can know?'

Adequate medical back up is essential at whatever level people are taking part in sport. 'Sport for all' can mean injury to many. The new National Sports Medicine Institute launched in 1992 will begin to provide a network of accredited centres across the UK.

We owe it to our aspiring **and** present international performers to have the best possible sports medicine services available to ensure they maximise their potential.

Consideration needs to be given to the provision of facilities for performance sport in two ways: making the best of what is available and planning for the future. It is vital that **all** facilities within a local area are managed effectively to maximise their use. New legislation regarding competitive tendering of local authority sports facilities and the management of schools will mean the development of new partnerships. Local strategies will need to be developed and actively pursued to ensure that there is coordination of these vital resources. Local authorities should be encouraged to review all facilities within their area and identify how these may best be used in the development of participation, performance and excellence. While accepting that nearly all facilities can provide a range of participation opportunities, it may be necessary to be more selective about developing performance 'specialisms' at each centre. The local strategy should identify 'performance centres' where improver groups and/or elite squads can work in the best possible environment. This will ensure that any investment in specialist equipment or building will not be duplicated unnecessarily. In order to allow participants using local facilities to improve their performance and to move towards national standard, sport in the UK requires a national network of specialist competition and/or training facilities distributed around the country.

Planning for performance includes allowing sufficient time in the facilities for training and competition. The amount of time needed for training will vary but performers should not find themselves always relegated to unsocial hours, as this can place intolerable demands on them and their families.

The time required to become a top flight performer is getting significantly greater. We have to address the problem of youngsters training for several hours each day in the swimming pool, the gymnasium or on the games field on top of a normal school day. We have all seen the pale faced swimmers at 6 am. in the local pool or the exhausted gymnast still training at 9 pm. at night. Sport has changed and if we wish to compete internationally, we have to consider new ways of releasing more time for our youngsters to train – changing the school timetable; providing residential schools of sport; offering university/college scholarships and so on. There are no easy solutions but we must ensure that our top class performers are not sacrificed because of inflexibility. For the facility manager there is always a difficult balance to strike between mass participation (good revenue) and performance development (less income), but the balance must be found if we are to provide opportunities for all members of the sporting community. What will happen to talented youngsters following competitive tendering? Will their battle for space and time become even greater?

Opportunity to develop talent does, of course, require more than the availability of facilities and time – often it requires transport. One of the most significant factors in performance development is the ability of the youngsters to get to the required training session. Should local authorities assist with transport to training venues or will we have to continue relying on the goodwill (and resources) of parents, coaches, youth leaders, etc.? In some European countries school buses or other means of public transport are used to shuttle youngsters to and from training throughout the year.

Having created the right environment, managing talent is critically important. The coach needs to establish a systematic way of monitoring and recording all useful data including:

- training schedules
- competition results
- injury records
- test results (fitness test, etc.)
- stress management record.

In order to do this, coaches need to establish a profiling system for each performer they work with to ensure they are 'tracked' successfully. Profiling will assist in three ways. It will help coaches to evaluate and motivate players at all levels, it will provide coaches with a framework for all round performer development and it will provide a standardised method of passing information on to other coaches.

The Lawn Tennis Association have established a player profiling system which includes a number of components – physical, mental, tactical, technical, matchplay results and external factors.

In conclusion, talent identification and development is a complex business which requires coordination, planning and resources. Substantial new resources are required in the UK if improvements are to be seen. With the emergence of the National Lottery there is optimism that new money will be available. However, this will only be successfully utilised through careful planning and cross agency cooperation.

*The greatest danger in life is not taking the risk to excel.*

**References**

(1991) **Intensive training centre programs.**
*Coaching Director* Vol 6, No 3, pp22-24.

Blincoe, Brian (1990) **The role of the county in the development of talent.**
*Coaches and Coaching* No 6, pp9-10.

Bohner, Wolfgang (1985) **Report of Womens Gymnastic Coaching Clinic.**
Bucharest, (Unpublished report)

Dent, Paul (1991) **Talent identification and selection.**
*Coaches and Coaching* No 8, pp3-5.

Dorrington, Annette (1986) **A visit to XI Shen School, Beijing.**
*Sports Coach* Vol 10, No 3, pp14-15.

Hahn, Allan G & Tumilty, Douglas McA (1989) **The rowing talent identification program – an outline.**
*EXCEL* Vol 5, No 3, pp12-14.

Kutsar, Kuulo (1991) **Hereditary prerequisites in the selection of potential talent.**
*Modern Athlete and Coach* Vol 29, No 1, pp12-14.

Kutsar, Kuulo (1991) **The Bulgarian sprints and hurdles system.**
*Modern Athlete and Coach* Vol 29, No 4, pp33-36.

Maylor, Christine (1987) **Talent development programme for netball to examine methods and results of Australian system in order to improve and refine existing regional programme with a view to development as a national scheme.**
(Unpublished report)

Olliver, Richard (1992) **The French spirit of training juniors.**
*Serve and Volley* Vol 11, No 3, pp77-78.

Preising, Wulf (1989) **Children in sport: a European perspective.**
*Sports Coach* Vol 12, No 3, pp27-31.

Samela, JH & Russell, SJ (1989) **The structure of knowledge in developing sport talent.**
Proceedings of the first IOC World Congress on Sport Sciences held in Colorado Springs, USA, October 28 – November 3 1989, pp370-74, Refs 2.

Schroter, Gerd & Voss Gerald (1991) **Predicting performances of young athletes.**
*Modern Athlete and Coach* Vol 29, No 3, pp26-29.

Tabachnik, Ben (1991) **Screening for talent.**
*Scholastic Coach* Vol 60, No 9, pp46-49, 76.

Telford, Richard D & Minikin, Brian R (1989) **The tri-level test for runners: a simple method of general fitness evaluation.**
*EXCEL* Vol 6, No 1, pp33-6, Refs 2.

Thissen-Milder, Mary & Mayhew, JL (1991) **Selection and classification of high school volleyball players from performance tests.**
*Journal of Sports Medicine and Physical Fitness* Vol 31, No 3, pp380-384, Refs 16.

Thomson, Rex W & Beavis, Noelle (1985) **Talent identification in sport.**
Report on behalf of the Otago University & Community Sports Trust for the New Zealand Sports Foundation Inc & The Ministry of Recreation and Sport.
Dunedin, New Zealand: University of Otago, pp196, Bibliog.

Woodman, Lawrie (1988) **Sport development: systems, trends and issues.**
*Coaching Director* Vol 4, No 2, pp4-12.

# Who Coaches the Coaches?

## Penny Crisfield

*Penny Crisfield joined the NCF in 1989 and is now Education Director, responsible for the development of resources and courses for coaches, tutors and assessors. She is Course Director of the Diploma in Coaching and currently involved in the development of a Certificate in Sports Coaching. She is also a member of the NCF National Faculty of Tutor Trainers and Assessors.*

## Introduction

> *By the year 1995, my guess is that more than 50% of people at work will recognise and benefit from systematic coaching.*

Parsloe, 1992

Eric Parsloe was not actually talking about sport when he made this prediction, but about business, and he was referring to changes in training and development in industry and the consequential changing role of supervisors and managers.

The quote sums up the dramatic changes in training which are happening across all occupations and throughout all segments of society. Whilst it might be argued that change is normal, there is no doubt that the pace of change has accelerated – typically people now move house more often, change jobs more frequently and try new sports more readily. Organisations re-structure more regularly, expand and contract more often, go into liquidation and re-establish more frequently. The same changes occur with ever increasing frequency in the economy and in technology, each imposing needs for rapid change in order to survive.

There have also been changes in the ethos of the process of education, training and development with passive learning, rote learning and formal exams becoming a thing of the past, and a shift towards laying greater responsibility upon managers; a stronger reliance upon vocational qualifications and competence-based assessment rather than specific training regimes. Training is becoming a much more competence-oriented activity and activities such as coaching, assessing and mentoring are now buzzwords in business as well as in sport.

Similar changes are going on in education institutions, as evidenced by initiatives such as the National Curriculum in schools and the likely development of a lead body in education to examine the development of vocational qualifications in education and teaching.

There are similar developments going on in sports coaching and coach education in response to the changes. If coaching is to make a real impact on society in general and the sporting opportunities of young people in particular, perhaps it must become more proactive and shape its own future. Stop to consider the potential impact of the coach on ten, fifty, even one hundred young people. The coach's coach has even greater impact, for by influencing even fifty coaches, they are ultimately affecting thousands of young sports people. In considering the coach's coach, we have an enormous responsibility to get it right and consequently there is a need to look carefully at the key question, who coaches the coaches? But first we need to consider a number of other questions. I think we need to ask ourselves why do coaches need coaching anyway? What do they need to be able to do?

**Why Coach the Coaches?**

Coaching is defined in the dictionary as tutoring, training, giving hints, priming; and these activities are generally deemed to enhance learning. Sports coaching is essentially a modern phenomenon and the early coaches were largely untrained and instinctive.

However, coaching in sport is now more widely accepted as a complex and far-reaching process which focuses on the fulfilment of the performer's needs rather than simply the acquisition of sports skills. Coaching might be seen along a continuum stretching from a hands-on instructional type of role at one end to a hands-off mentoring type of role at the other (not unlike the differing role of the driving instructor who at one end is operating with learner drivers and using dual-controls, and the other is honing the expertise of the Nigel Mansells).

instructing
(hands-on)

mentoring
(hands-off)

Towards the left hand end of the continuum, the coaching might be closely aligned with teaching and possibly confined to one-off sessions or a short period of instruction. For example, the novice undergoing their first experience of archery is likely to receive instruction on how to stand, knock the arrow, hold the bow, raise and aim, and shoot. As you move towards the right hand end, there is a shift towards a more prolonged and comprehensive relationship between coach and performer. This would be more like the relationship between coach and national squad archer.

Irrespective of the degree of hands-on/hands-off type of coaching, we would probably accept that a central concern of the quality coach is with the total growth of the performer through the improvement of performance and the development of skills. This requires some planned, systematic process, toward some clearly defined goals; with continuous monitoring and evaluation. There will also be a range of less readily defined characteristics which are to do with personal skills and values. Within the NCF, we frequently describe the characteristics of the quality coach as: caring, craft and commitment.

It must be possible to identify the necessary knowledge and skills required by the coach to accelerate this growth within the performer. We should therefore accept that it is possible to facilitate the development of these coaching competencies through some form of training and education. Coach training is a fairly recent upshot and in the past was confined to conveying knowledge of the sports (its rules, techniques and tactics). It is now recognised as a key component of effective coaching and so we must ask: what to coach the coaches?

## What to Coach the Coaches?

With the emergence of standards for coaching instituted by NCVQ, it is now quite clear what coaches need to be able to do. In essence, these standards delineate a series of tasks which coaches should be able to undertake successfully – tasks which essentially incorporate the heart of the coaching process, and to some extent determine the coach's role:

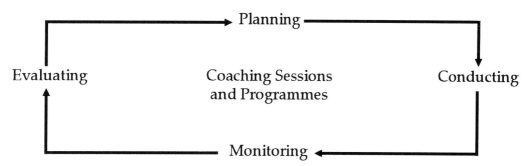

To be able to achieve these tasks, it is possible to identify a range of knowledge and skills which are required. For example, within the global task of planning, we might identify skills such as:

- collecting information to plan and prepare a session
- preparing facilities and equipment.

We might also identify essential knowledge of, for example:

- the individual's needs, current state of fitness, technical skills, etc.
- training principles
- facility needs, safe operations, access etc.

Within the task of conducting coaching sessions, we might identify skills such as:

- presenting skills and techniques within the activity
- providing feedback on performance.

We might also identify essential knowledge of, for example:

- demonstrations, stages of skill acquisition
- type of feedback, timing of feedback etc.

Of course, none of this is new, merely organised more logically and brought more clearly to our attention through the development of the coaching NVQ standards. It is apparent that the depth and breadth of knowledge available is increasing – you have only to think of developments in exercise physiology, nutrition, psychological skills training, sports medicine and equipment design. Essentially there is more content. The range of skills required by the modern day coach is extensive (perhaps expanding as the professionalisation of coaching takes place). Think of the growing expertise in communication skills training and management training (and the recent initiative of the Sports Council, *Running Sport*). In other words, there is more to learn about the process, as well as more content.

This tells us about what coaches need to learn but not how they learn.

**How Do Coaches Learn?**

Once we have clearly identified what skills and knowledge are necessary, we need to consider how coaches can gain these, and how they learn. We might suggest that people learn through the interaction of theory/principles and experience/practice. Learning is really about creating change and this is only likely to happen if the coach is motivated to embark on the process of:

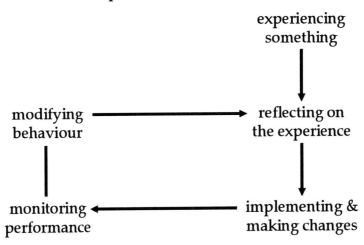

Most adults have learnt the art of switching off rather than switching on to the learning process. Perhaps the same is true of coaches, even when they are embarking on training courses. We know that learning does not happen immediately and that we cannot readily determine whether people have learnt or not. It is about a change in behaviour or attitude; and again this takes time. How far does this happen on NGB coach training courses? How do you know that you have influenced the coach's behaviour? How do you know the coach is ready to change? I believe that too often we hope we are having an effect, but too often our methods don't necessarily switch the coach on to learning. They switch them off or attempt to switch them on to a prescribed format for coaching performers (perhaps the NGB way).

The coach's coach needs to understand how they might be able to effect these sort of changes; and there are obviously a whole host of ways by which coaches might learn:

- Through some form of self coaching.
- By trial and error, which is the basis of many training programmes but which can be time consuming and may not result in improvements.
- By observing others, which may be very powerful, providing the person is a good example. It may of course happen unconsciously so we need to be careful.
- By coaching manuals, text books, videos and tapes, which may provide a sound basis and build confidence but are unlikely to develop practical coaching competence.
- By analysing performers and the demands of the sport.

Any of these may be enhanced with coaching from others by:

- attending a course from a tutor/coach (eg. NGB)
- studying a course through home learning
- co-coaching
- working under the guidance of a coach/mentor.

In trying to determine which mode might be the most effective, we would probably conclude that it would depend upon:

- the specific situation
- what is to be learnt
- the preference of the coach. It is important to recognise that people have different ways of learning (ie. different learning styles – visualisers, verbalisers, listeners, writers etc.)
- the quality of the experience (eg. the course, the tutor, the text).

Some methods might be more efficient but each has its own merits in the right situation, and indeed a combination of methods might be most effective anyway. Whatever method or range of methods, one of the key things to appreciate is that coaches learn most effectively when they:

- are building upon their own experience and knowledge
- can see the relevance and value to their own practice
- can readily use the information or ideas in their own practice.

Again I challenge you to examine your own training programmes and consider the extent to which these learning principles underpin the methods that you use to train your coaches. Perhaps you may feel you have the 'what' right but has sufficient time been invested in the 'how'? How is as important as what.

**How to Coach Coaches**

Irrespective of the method of coaching, I believe there are three components when considering how. We need to consider:

- first the outcome (ie. what coaches should be able to do at the end, based on their current knowledge and experience)
- then the process (how we can best provide learning opportunities that help the coach to achieve the outcome)
- then identifying the need to know content which will enable them to maximise the learning opportunities and achieve the outcome.

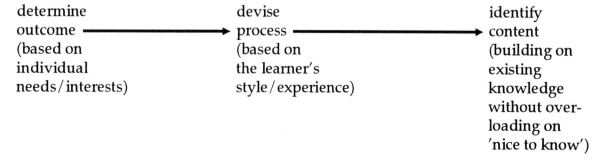

| determine outcome (based on individual needs/interests) | → | devise process (based on the learner's style/experience) | → | identify content (building on existing knowledge without over-loading on 'nice to know') |
|---|---|---|---|---|

The outcome may be an attitude or behaviour change, the acquisition of skill or knowledge. The outcome must accommodate the needs and interests of the coach (remember we have to switch them on to the learning process); and determine the content. The process must render the content meaningful and relevant. It must also interact with the coach's preferred learning style. The issue therefore is how can the coach's coach create an effective learning environment, in which they build on the coach's experience, elucidate the relevance and facilitate their application? I am convinced that this means starting at the coach and at their coaching (at their knowledge and experience, which is often far more extensive than either the trainer or the coach recognise), rather than starting at the body of knowledge. This places the emphasis as strongly (if not more strongly) on the delivery or process skills of the coach's coach, rather than their level of specialist/technical expertise. Inevitably it is a balance, for the coach's coach must:

- have the necessary knowledge/technical expertise
- have coaching experience and credibility to be able to build the bridge between theory and practice
- have the teaching and communication skills and experience to help others acquire this knowledge and develop these skills (understanding of the learning process and learning styles, principles of adult learning, group processes and intervention skills)
- provide an appropriate role model
- have the motivation, time and commitment to coach coaches
- know what it takes to become an effective coach.

My bias would be towards the 'how' skills rather than the 'what' skills, for the essence of any educational process is in developing self-analytical and reflective skills, facilitating application and creating the desire to find out more, rather than simply cramming knowledge. Returning to the outcome-process-content model, note that the role of the coach's coach is to facilitate learning through a process that makes the content meaningful, challenging and relevant. Their effectiveness is dependent upon their ability to centre the learning on the coach's needs and interests; and guide them towards the attainment of agreed outcomes (ie. support them to change their coaching behaviour).

Again I ask you to reflect on your own process of training coaches and the role that you ask the coach's coach to play. Of course there are many ways, and I think the role of the coach's coach is likely to expand and indeed change, in the light of the changing world of education and coach education:

**Deliverer of taught courses**
Typically the coach's coach has been employed to be the deliverer of taught courses. The effectiveness of taught courses is largely dependent upon the facilitatory skills of the tutor to assess the needs and experience of individuals, match their learning styles through a process which renders the content relevant, meaningful and applicable.

The danger can be that it becomes a one way interaction in which the coach's coach gives the coach new information, which although interesting, may not enable them to use it in their own coaching (ie. it may not result in changes in behaviour, in true learning). I fear what too frequently happens is that a coach attends the course, enjoys it, gains new information, places the new information on the shelf, and returns to their tried and tested coaching practice. They have not been helped to analyse their own behaviour nor supported whilst they try new things; then monitor, evaluate and modify their coaching practice.

Taught courses can sometimes create a conflict between meeting the coach's specific needs and providing sufficient course standardisation to ensure the necessary quality control. I think this can be overcome by the development of tutor packs which prescribe the course outcomes (ie. the standardisation) whilst providing sufficient flexibility on the approach and the emphasis.

### Supporter of independent learning

This may well become a future role of the coach's coach as the popularity of home learning materials increases. Home study packs are convenient (they enable coaches to work in their own time and at their own pace), and can provide a very effective learning medium for some coaches. Evidence suggests that ideally they need human support (ie. some additional coaching to enable the coach to transfer and apply the skills and knowledge of their own coaching). This might be achieved by offering tutorial support or by building on the packs on subsequent taught courses and workshops.

### Mentor

This is perhaps one of the more recent and growing roles of the coach's coach. The word mentor is derived from a character from Greek mythology who was a wise and trusted adviser and counsellor, and is now used to refer to a role which incorporates the concepts of apprenticeship, counselling, facilitating and role modelling. It is becoming a highly popular form of training within both business and education, as well as coaching. The fundamental skills of mentoring are summed up in words such as: support, guide, facilitate, motivate, listen, question and enable. Words such as assess, tell, direct and restrict, are generally agreed to fall outside the role of the mentor.

A number of governing bodies are developing mentoring schemes whereby less experienced coaches are teamed up with more experienced coaches. This is a fascinating interaction for without doubt, both can learn from each other. At present the system is somewhat haphazard in so far as its effectiveness is dependent upon the skills of the mentor. It is vital that we learn from other arenas with greater experience of mentoring and draw up guidelines and frameworks for both training and operation.

### Assessor

Increasingly, the coach's coach will be required to determine whether or not the coach can coach, to make the assessment. With the development of NVQ standards for coaching, tutors are likely to take on the role of assessor, which is to check a coach's skills against a list of competencies. The role is similar to that of the driving test examiner, who checks that the learner driver is able to manoeuvre the car in a number of ways and is familiar with the rules of the road. Assessment should take place in the workplace (ie. at the track, by the pool, on the field), in the same way as the driving test examiner tests on the roads rather than in some test centre. The assessor's role will include observation, questioning and evaluation supporting evidence (eg. a coach's log). It is likely to become an integral part of the training process and consequently the tutor may well also need to be trained as an assessor.

Having addressed the issue about why coach the coaches, and what and how to coach the coaches, now we can turn to the question, 'who coaches the coaches?'.

## Who Coaches the Coaches?

The best coach of coaches must be coaches themselves but this assumes that all coaches have the necessary skills that were identified before. We must be careful not to make the same erroneous assumptions that people have made with regard to performers. Good performers do not necessarily make good coaches and good coaches will not necessarily make good coaches of coaches (nor necessarily good mentors). Having the necessary underpinning knowledge about coaching and experience of the process of coaching is simply not enough.

The coach's coach need not always be a technical expert in everything they coach. They certainly need to be able to listen, ask the right questions, understand the problem and provide positive feedback. Who is best placed to do this?

Ideally selected and trained coaches from within the governing body who can fulfil the criteria laid down earlier. There may also be a role for some coach educators, who are not necessarily experts in the particular sport, but who have technical expertise in more generic areas and most importantly the identified process skills. Whichever source, there is a need to train the coach's coach or we risk haphazard, diverse and ineffectual learning. We won't switch the coach on to the learning process and what they gain is left too much to chance, and what they use is likely to be still more hit-or-miss.

## How Do We Coach the Coach's Coach?

The National Coaching Foundation has recognised that the training of the coach's coach is the key to the provision of a quality coach education programme. The logic goes like this: if we believe that the provision of a quality sports experience at every level (foundation, participation, performance and excellence) is dependent upon quality coaching, then to develop a quality coach (caring, craft and commitment) demands a quality training programme, which in turn demands a quality coach's coach, which in turn demands a quality training programme for the coach's coach.

What does this mean?

- Careful selection in the first instance. Currently we look for sound interpersonal skills, experience in and empathy for coaching, specialist and current knowledge. Ideally, we also look for tutoring experience and facilitation skills. Within the NCF system, this is ascertained through informal interview and scrutiny of pro formas. In the near future, it will also include a short assessment to check on specialist knowledge.
- Completion of a home study pack to provide information on adult learning principles, interactive tutoring skills and presentation skills.
- Successful completion of a 2-day workshop which includes two presentations to small groups with a comprehensive debriefing session and inputs about the philosophies of coach education methods and the role of assessment.

- A period of apprenticeship during which the tutor works with an experienced tutor and co-tutors (the forerunner of the tutor's mentor).

- A probationary period during which the tutor's effectiveness is carefully monitored, culminating in their appointment as an NCF staff tutor.

This is the current state of the art but it will require ongoing development. For example, there is:

- a need to assist tutors to support coaches who are undertaking home learning packs

- as yet inadequate in-service training for tutors (available in 1993)

- as yet no assessor training to enable the coach's coach to become an NVQ assessor (available in 1993)

- as yet no provision to assist the coach's coach in their mentoring role (available in 1993)

- a need for collaboration between the professional body, the NGBs and the NCF to provide the sort of training provision which will best serve the NGBs and the coaches.

## Conclusion

We know that the coach's coach has enormous potential impact on coaches and ultimately on the quality of sports opportunities in this country. I believe we must invest in the coach's coach now. We must look ahead and be proactive, for we are living in a changing world in communication, knowledge, education, technology, sport and social climate. The challenge we must meet is to enable the coach's coach to help the coach to synthesise and integrate these changes, to improve the quality of sports performance and the enjoyment of sport for all ages and all performance levels. The responsibility for the quality of tomorrow's coaches lies in our hands.

# Influencing the Child's Lifestyle

## Roger Davis

*Roger Davis trained as a PE teacher and was Head of Physical Education at a large mixed comprehensive school in Coventry, and an assistant youth leader for twelve years. He led the Sports Council's National Demonstration Project 'Active Lifestyles', promoting school to community links. He joined the Sports Council's Development Unit in 1991 with responsibility for young people and sport. He is an active rugby and cricket coach and enjoys outdoor pursuits.*

### Introduction

This paper will lean on the evidence of the Active Lifestyles National Demonstration Project in Coventry and consider how – from an education / sport base – we can influence young people's lifestyles. Active Lifestyles' unique starting point was from the curriculum. The key message was one of partnership and co-ordination. The presentation suggested that the opportunities to work collaboratively at a local level are still relevant, even more so in times of change with scarce resources.

Let's identify some of the issues of working in this way, and remember this personal statement of faith, 'more young people playing more sport, more of the time'.

Some paradoxes became apparent from yesterday's presentations. Yes, pathways to excellence are necessary but unless school and community get it right, the rest may not follow.

Concern was expressed that the TOYA Project highlighted the need for supportive parents. Do all young people have access to sporting opportunities in this sense, and if not, why not?

'Sport for All' is a turn-off for many. Young people's leisure is 'up for grabs'; the youth culture perpetuates pop and fashion, and sport has to compete.

How important is sport to young people? Are structures in place for young people to access sporting opportunity, and are parents, teachers, and coaches suitably trained to be child sensitive? It is hoped that the Coventry model highlights opportunities for you all to play your part with teachers in the provision of a 'common youth sport policy'.

The evidence is reassuring. Young people are switched on to sport.

You may not all be aware of the origins of the Active Lifestyles project. It was created in 1984 and continued to 1991, and was a partnership between Coventry City Council and the Sports Council (West Midlands?). The main area of concern was to ensure that young people would be able to participate in post-school sport (14-18 year olds).

*Question:* What will young people take with them from school to community?

*Answer:* Knowledge, skills and understanding, and the desire to remain active throughout life.

Schools have a role to play in preparing young people for post school opportunities; they should be physically literate and independently active.

A relevant curriculum should include the following three areas:

**Health related fitness**
Concern for young people's fitness/activity levels. Units of work designed to teach young people about their bodies, and to provide appropriate activity within the context of school and community.

**Education for active leisure**
Remove barriers to participation; arrange centre visits; provide information, market opportunities, set up a database. Arrange introductions to places and organisations with provision for young people. Include local coaches and provide realistic opportunities to return.

**Community provision – what's available**
For example, visits to leisure services facilities; providing new activities on site; group coaching off-site; extend existing curriculum activities; sports specific development schemes; girls in clubs.

**Teachers as Role Models**

The issues are broader here, with PE in the curriculum leading to sports development in the community. The SDO network and professional coaches should be involved in working to encourage lifelong activity, thus forming a structural link and fostering good relationships. A motivational link will be established through the changing attitudes of young people towards activity, and a contextual link in terms of young people's experience.

Teachers should reflect on their methods, for example:

- How much do they know about their own pupils, and their opinions of the PE experience?
- Their involvement out of school, significant patterns in their introduction and eventual participation, attitudes and knowledge.
- Which sports they liked or disliked and why?
- Was this approach successful with regard to young people's on-going participation?

The traditional view of mass post-school drop-out was a myth. The results of the 1985-88 postal survey of 1000 pupils showed a drop-off in many sports, but shifting interests; in the main, a physically active population predisposed to activity.

A wide breadth of experience is required at Key Stages 3/4, so there are opportunities for the sporting network of clubs and SDOs to play their part. Are participation/performance structures in place?

A small proportion wanted to try a new sport, but there were difficulties including: cost, work, poor facilities, lack of enjoyment and people to play with. A significant number participated in sport on a casual, unintentional basis, and even the negative played something. Many young people were involved in the arts and music. Most intended to take up club based activities, but there was little success in this area. Why?

There will be opportunities for similar work in the future, but recognised changes in education, the national curriculum, PE, LMS, and limited in-service opportunities, could lead to a key stage overload.

## Opportunities

- Key Stage 4, non statutory guidance notes and curriculum guidance.
- Curriculum Guidance Note 5 (Health Education), LMS, marketing your school, marketing sport, community use of school sites.
- In-service, schools free to choose, one-to-one working.

## Further Opportunities

- Cross-phase 5-16, joint inset, education/sport interface.

There is a growing interest in youth sport, as indicated by the *Young People and Sport Policy Document* which specifies the Sports Council's aims and objectives for achieving a better sports experience for young people. The document calls for a collective effort by all agencies and individuals who influence the sporting development of young people by providing guidance through 'frameworks for action'.

## The Future

The following needs were identified:

- Co-ordination at school.
- Staff responsible at a local level (Youth Sport Manager).
- Club-school liaison.
- National governing bodies – common youth sport policy.

In conclusion, we should all be aware that young people are our common concern, and that partnership does work. What part can you play in influencing young people's lifestyle?

# Performance Planning – What is it?

## Katie Donovan

*A native of the United States of America and formerly Director of the American Coaching Effectiveness Program in Champaign, Illinois, Katie Donovan is now Director of Development at the National Coaching Foundation. She is responsible for Tutor and Assessor Training, and also for Champion Coaching, the youth sport and coach development initiative.*

**Three Major Objectives Should Underpin Performance Planning:**

1 **To provide a structure for the specialist development of individual performers.**
This should include information on the following topics:

- Talent identification programmes.
- Talent development programmes.
- Competitive structures.
- International competition.
- Award schemes.
- Facilities.

2 **To provide a systematic and programmed education for coaches.**
This should include information on the following topics:

- Coach recruitment.
- Content and levels of coach education programmes.
- Quality control mechanisms.
- Monitoring and updating of coaches.
- Employment and deployment of coaches.

3 **To provide and/or co-ordinate the appropriate support services for performers and coaches at all levels.**
This should include information on the following topics:

- Fitness testing and monitoring.
- Psychological counselling and support.
- Nutritional information and advice.
- Movement/match analysis.
- Sports medicine support.

**Questions to be Answered**

1 **To provide a structure for the specialist development of individual performers**
*Talent identification programmes*

- Does the sport have a 'profiling' system for performers (ie. are records kept on individual performers)?
- Has the sport got access to information on profiles of top performers from other countries?
- How does the sport identify talented performers at this present time? (This should be linked to competitive structures, centres of excellence, elite squad training, etc.).
- Does the sport have good links with schools?
- Does the sport provide training for school teachers and coaches to assist with talent identification?
- Does the sport have a register of local clubs, where suitably trained 'youth' coaches operate, which could be made available to schools?

*Talent development programmes*

- Does the sport have a clearly defined 'ladder' of talent development?
- Are talented junior performers developed largely through:
  - clubs?
  - schools?
  - other agencies? Please specify.
- Does the sport have regional youth training squads/centres of excellence for young performers?
- How are young people selected for these squads and at what age? Please specify.
- Does the sport have national squad training for top young performers?
- How are young people selected for these squads and at what age?
- Does the sport provide any bridges for top young performers to help them cross into senior squads/competition?

*Competition structures*

- At what age are competitions introduced?
- What are the major competitive age divisions in the sport?
- How are competitions structured in the sport?
  eg: local, regional, national
  or club, country, national.
- At what age do performers begin competing internationally?

*International competition*

- What international teams does the sport have?
- In what major championships will the sport compete in over the next four years? Please specify dates and venues.
- What other overseas competitions do the sport feel are important in the development of performers over the next four years. State **why** they are significant. Give all relevant dates and venues.
- Does the sport require 'special' training camps in the next four years (eg. warm weather training, altitude training)?

*Award schemes*

- What award schemes are available in the sport?
- Who are the schemes targeted at?
- Who, if anyone, sponsors it?
- What way does it help achieve the overall objectives of the sport?

| Name of Award Scheme | Sponsors | Target Population | How does it help achieve objectives? |
|---|---|---|---|

*Facilities*

- Does the sport largely operate using private premises or public facilities?
- Does the sport require purpose-built facilities?
- Does the sport have a national training centre?
- Does the sport have the facilities to stage major competitions in the UK?
- Does the sport have blueprints available for local authorities to guide them on the type of facility required?

2  **To provide a systematic and programmed education for coaches**
*Coach recruitment*

- Does the sport need more coaches?
- Does the sport need more coaches to work with:
  - novice performers?
  - improver groups?
  - high level performers?
- Where do the majority of coaches come from in the sport: eg. parents, teachers, ex-competitors etc.
- Does the sport have a positive recruitment campaign to encourage new people to take up coaching? Please specify.
- Does the sport have a leader's award?

*Content and levels of coach education programmes*

- How many levels of award does the sport have? Please specify each award and indicate the broad areas of study included:

| Name of Award | | Content | |
|---|---|---|---|
| Technical Sports Specific | Organisational Methodology | Performance Related (eg. Fitness Mental Prep etc.) | Vocational |

- What use is made of National Coaching Foundation programmes or other educational resources? Please specify.
- Is specific training given to those working with 'junior' performers on topics such as child growth and development?
  YES / NO Please specify.
- Does the sport have clear assessment criteria for skills, knowledge and experience of coaches at all levels of the award structure?

*Quality control mechanisms*

- Does the sport have any tutor training for people conducting coaching award courses?
- Does the sport provide standardised resource materials to support awarded courses?
- Are the courses available at the same standard throughout the country?
- Does the sport have a national strategy for the implementation of the award programme?

*Monitoring and updating of coaches*

- Does the sport have a register of **active** coaches?
- Does the sport know how many coaches they have at each level? If so please specify.
- Does the sport have any system of monitoring the work of qualified coaches?
- Does the sport make any provision for the periodic updating/re-training of their coaches?

*Employment and deployment of coaches*

- Does the sport provide legislation to ensure that only qualified coaches work within their competitive and organisational structures?
- Does the sport provide recommendations for the relationships between qualification and remuneration?
- Does the sport provide clear parameters within which coaches at different levels can and should operate?

- Does the sport have clear pathways of development for coaches – voluntary and professional?
- Is the deployment of coaches – voluntary and professional – clearly structured and well managed?
- Does the sport liaise closely with local authorities to ensure that the standards in the sport are maintained?

3 **To provide and/or co-ordinate the appropriate support services for performers and coaches at all levels.**

*Fitness testing and monitoring*

- Does the sport have a clear policy with regard to fitness training for young performers (eg. use of weights)?
- Does the sport have any standard field testing procedures for performers (ie. non-laboratory)?
- Does the sport have relevant data on the various aspects of fitness necessary for high level performance – endurance, strength, speed, flexibility?
- Are the high level performers regularly tested and monitored? If yes, specify where the testing is done, by whom and how frequently.
- Is any research being carried out on a particular aspect of physiological preparation for sport? If yes, specify the nature of the research, where it is being done and by whom.

*Psychological counselling and support*

- Is mental preparation an important part of the sport?
- Do the coaches in the sport include mental training as part of their normal training programmes?
- At what age is mental preparation introduced for performers?
- Does the sport use (on a voluntary or professional basis) a sports psychologist to work with their coaches and/or performers. Specify what level, frequency and status.

*Nutritional information and advice*

- Does the sport have particular nutritional needs (ie. weight loss, weight gain)?
- Who 'administers' any nutritional advice (eg. team doctor, physiotherapist, dietitian)?
- Are there known strategies in the sport for pre-competition and post-competition diets? Please specify.
- Does the sport have access to dietary analysis for performers?

*Movement/match analysis*

- Does the sport require **detailed** movement analysis (eg. gymnastics, diving, trampolining)?
- Does the sport require **detailed** match analysis (eg. soccer, basketball, volleyball)?
- How much is known of studies conducted elsewhere in the world?
- What use is made of computers in analysing movement or match play?

*Sports medicine support*

- Does the sport actively encourage medical screening for its top level performers? If so, where and when is this carried out?
- Does the sport have a medical officer? If so, give details.
- Does the sport have ready access to a physiotherapist at:
    - national level?
    - regional level?
    - local level?
- Does a doctor attend squad training sessions?
- Does a doctor travel with teams abroad?
- Does a physiotherapist attend squad training sessions?
- Does a physiotherapist travel with teams abroad?
- Does the sport have a rehabilitation programme for injured performers?
- How does the sport implement drug testing?

# Champion Coaching: A Case Study

## Phyl Edwards

*Phyl Edwards is a qualified physical education teacher who has taught and lectured at IM Marsh College, Liverpool, and at Liverpool Polytechnic. She is currently head of SDS Ltd, an educational consultancy whose regular clients include the Department of Education and Science, the Sports Council, the National Coaching Foundation and the Lawn Tennis Association. A former England Netball International and panel coach, she is also a professional squash coach and examiner, and a senior athletics coach.*

### Introduction

The first phase of Champion Coaching was launched on 1 April 1991. In twelve months it had made such an impact on sport for young people that it was not only granted further funding of 1.3 million pounds from the Foundation for Sport and the Arts, but has also been awarded the Queen's Gold award for services to the community.

Notwithstanding its success it would only be fair to say that the first phase had a number of shortcomings, some of which could be described as teething problems, others which were as a result of either errors of judgement or a misunderstanding of specific situations.

It must also be emphasized that Champion Coaching had to be implemented within a six month time frame, and the shortness of time had an understandable impact on the first phase of the project.

### Champion Coaching Shortcomings

#### Governing body veto
The National Governing Bodies had too little say in which sports were placed in which scheme. One example was Hockey which was included in one of the shire country schemes, when monitoring surveys showed that at local level the GBs knew that the exit routes were full, and that junior membership in local clubs was virtually impossible to obtain. However, this situation had not been checked out prior to sport acceptance and hence at the end of the scheme the children were unable to continue with the sport.

#### Governing body selected coaches
Some governing bodies were a little concerned that certain of their coaches were rejected on the grounds that they could not attend the coach education weekends. While it was accepted that quality assurance was a key feature of the programme, it might have been more acceptable if some discretion had been used in this matter, especially when some of the reasons for non-attendance were perfectly legitimate.

## Coach education

The second minor problem concerning the coach education weekends was not only that they were compulsory, but were scheduled at the beginning of September. Many GBs have their county trials at that time, and hence many coaches had to make the decision whether they would attend trials or the weekend training. This may have had something to do with the poor reception for the weekend from the netball coaches, some of whom felt their first duty was to attend county trials.

## Inappropriate Selection of Schemes and Participants

### Schemes

Some schemes were just not ready for Champion Coaching, or had actually applied for the wrong motives, ie. to 'take the money and run'. This was difficult to judge on the first run through, and such schemes were for the most part rooted out prior to Phase Two. Any of the schemes who felt that they would get something for nothing were much mistaken. Champion Coaching in this instance exemplified the saying 'nothing without work', and many of the Scheme Liaison Officers (SLOs) were under an unacceptable amount of stress caused by the workloads. In many schemes the local authority had to support their work with additional administrative support at their own expense. Had there been more set up time, a more exact screening process could have been carried out which could have flagged up warnings for both partners.

### Participants

The selection of the participants was, to a large extent, left to the SLOs to implement. The methods varied from PE teachers asking children, 'Who wants to take part?', to full trials, to an elite squad containing overseas players in the country on sport scholarships. Some coaches complained that the children were of too low a skill level, while some were obviously too advanced for the scheme, and in fact the risk over playing for such children was obvious. Again, far more thought should have been given to this aspect.

## The Alienation of the PE Profession

The alienation of the PE profession was a cardinal and almost fatal mistake. The initial feeling was that the PE profession had abdicated all responsibility for after-school sport. The first few visits to schemes' PE Workshops gave the lie to this opinion. Later in the scheme the problem was rectified, and the fact that professional bodies and the inspectorate put their weight behind Champion Coaching helped to turn the tide. However, it was obvious to the monitoring team that where PE was supporting the scheme there was a different approach and attitude prevailing, and for the most part these schemes showed productive links between the schools, the advisers and the SLOs.

## The Coach Education Programme

The coach education programme was too intensive, with too much information being presented in a short space of time, and almost totally reliant on face to face contact for delivery. There were criticisms of the weekends, many of which were absolutely justified. However, for those coaches who were not used to working with children they were essential, and many such coaches expressed their satisfaction with both method and content of the programme. The main criticism came from teachers/coaches who had already covered most of this work at college, yet no exemptions were given for professional qualifications. There was also a suggestion that it might have been better to have provided the training for assistant coaches, many of whom felt that they needed a great deal of help which was not provided. A further suggestion was that the head coach should cascade training down to the other scheme coaches. However, time constraints meant that this was not a viable option, but the local support of assistant coaches was a scheme weakness.

## Too Many Free Materials?

There was a feeling amongst some schemes that there was too much free material provided for coaches, parents and children. To a certain extent this criticism was justified, but if Champion Coaching is thought of as a new product launch, then it becomes not only understandable, but justifiable. It has been suggested that the high profile of the scheme achieved by the use of these promotional materials led to relatively high levels of publicity both locally and nationally, all of which made a large contribution to the success of the fund raising for the second phase, and the vastly increased funding granted at the end of the first phase. If this was the case then the money was well spent.

There were also some criticisms from certain SLOs of the unit cost of the schemes. However, many of these were based on experience of having run holiday schemes, and Champion Coaching was not that type of exercise. The high ratio of coaches to children, plus the excellence of the venues marked the scheme out as a quality, and hence relatively expensive product.

## Assistant Coaches

One of the main weaknesses of Phase One was the treatment of the assistant coaches, who appeared to get very little from the scheme relative to some of the other groups. However, very few truly came into this category, and while head coaches received a £200 honorarium, many assistant coaches were paid at local authority rates with at least one example of an assistant coach being paid fees in excess of any payment to head coaches.

However, it was acknowledged that more should have been done for the assistant coaches to thank them for their loyalty, and give them greater identity with the scheme. Some SLOs did in fact take the initiative and provide T-shirts for assistant coaches, but this was not required as an official part of the scheme.

## Exit Routes, Fact or Fiction?

Exit routes were often ill thought out and badly planned, and in fact some simply did not exist. In some instances the schemes created their own; this was not under the direction of Champion Coaching but the initiative of the head coach and/or SLO.

## Too Much Paper in the System?

There was too much paper in the system. Fact, and no excuses.

## The Logs

It was considered by many SLOs and coaches that both the logs were too complicated. Again, this was true; but there were some coaches who felt that the Coaches Log was useful in that it assisted the planning process. Others felt it took too much time to complete, and required too much unnecessary information. The answer was probably somewhere in between. Logs are an essential adjunct to a coach's work, but for maximum usage they need to be absolutely user friendly and as quick and easy to complete as possible, and the Coaches Log of Phase One was certainly neither of these.

The childrens' SportLog was a good idea, but a serious case of overkill, and I personally did not see one which had even half the sections with information recorded. Again, the logs were a good idea, but they took a great deal of time to explain, and to check if they were being maintained, and the use of this time needed to be measured against the purpose for which the child was intended to keep the log. If they were considered for use as records of achievement then the detail would have required much more refinement. As they stood, the logs in their original form must give rise to some debate about their value.

## Monitoring and Evaluation

The monitoring and evaluation lacked any real objective data, and had no long term process in-built, so that having completed the scheme all work came to an end. This was understandable in that there was no guarantee that there would be a long term future for the scheme, and therefore to plan an ongoing process was futile. However, the argument made for the inclusion of hard data was one which was lost, with some resultant criticism from individuals who were looking for a valid, statistical analysis of the results.

## Champion Coaching – The Strengths

The strengths of Champion Coaching far outweighed its weaknesses, and the groups which could be said to have benefited most from these strengths were the:

- coaches
- children
- Governing Bodies of Sport.

### The coaches
Coaches for the most part were very happy with the scheme (logs excepted). One of the major plus points was that they had little or no administration to undertake. They did not have to book the hall, order the coach, collect the children. In fact all they had to do was to turn up and coach.

Their planning was made very easy, because scheme liaison officers had taken most of the burdens from them, and despite all the complaints the logs helped with course structure and evaluation.

All the equipment and venues were supplied, and although not all the equipment was top of the range there was always sufficient to operate safely and effectively, and if more was needed the SLO would do their best to supply it from other sources.

The venues at which the schemes took place were, with few exceptions, excellent and far better than most coaches, local authorities or clubs could have afforded if working on their own.

In fact the coaches had a complete in-built support structure, and probably for the first time in their lives all they had to do was what they do best... COACH.

### The children
Without exception the children and their parents felt that they had gained much from scheme participation. I did not interview one parent who felt that the children had not benefited from participating in Champion Coaching.

The children felt that they had improved their personal skill levels.

The scheme encouraged disciplined commitment to sport, and the emphasis on fair play was considered to be a very important feature.

One of the most often quoted benefits was the fact that they had made new friends, or had met up with friends they had previously had at primary school. Some parents also felt that the scheme was opening up new groups of friends with an interest in sport, and this was considered beneficial.

In terms of skill learning it helped children to appreciate not only their own ability, but also to recognise and respect ability in others.

Possibly the most important aspect as far as the children were concerned was that they had fun, and would very much like to repeat the experience.

### The Governing Bodies
The Governing Bodies were given the opportunity to examine their own youth sport policies, something which many of them had not done prior to Champion Coaching. It allowed them to consider the role of those coaches who wish to specialise in working with children. It opened up, for many sports, a new pool of prospective talent from which future elite athletes may be drawn. Finally, it pointed the need for a register of coaches in that many governing bodies could not readily advise SLOs on the availability of coaches working in their area.

### Summary

Champion Coaching had an impact on all of those who took part:

- It gave a new dimension to after school sport, with more support for PE staff, and increased choice for children.
- It introduced the concept of local audits of youth sport, something which had never been done on such a scale before.
- It helped to build bridges between physical education and sport.
- It gave birth to local Youth Sport Action Groups
- It gave the PE professionals a new perspective on the training of teachers, and the new breed of 'Youth Sport Co-ordinators' are currently in training.
- It provided an ideal assessment centre for governing bodies to assess candidates for S/NVQs.
- It helped to produce a new breed of coach – **The Children's Coach.**

Champion Coaching had some major advantages over many of the excellent youth sport schemes which were already running throughout the country. Perhaps most important was its strong links with the NCF, and the additional resources which were available as a result of this. It was also relatively well financed, far more so than any other scheme I have monitored.

It also had disadvantages; not enough staff, and it had to be put together in record time at a difficult time of the year. Nevertheless, it had a dedicated team of workers and was ably led by Katie Donovan.

It has been said that Champion Coaching is 'but one tree in a forest'. This is undoubtedly true, but it is a tree which has now established roots, and one which should in time produce some strong saplings which will continue the growth of the forest, and provide a firm platform on which to build the future of youth sport in this country.

# Partnerships Aren't Easy

## Steve Grainger

*Steve Grainger is Champion Coaching Officer with the National Coaching Foundation, with responsibility for building up partnerships with local authorities to assist them in their delivery of youth sport and coach development programmes. Prior to taking up this post in June 1992 he was Principal Officer (Sport) with Nottinghamshire County Council Leisure Services.*

The dictionary definition of partnership is that of 'A contractual relationship between two or more persons carrying on a joint business venture with a view to profit, each incurring liability for losses and the right to share in the profits'.

This could be applied to sport but in a sports development sense I prefer to look at partnership as a process of Communication (talking to others), Cooperation (working together with those others) and Coordination (working together in a planned, structured, agreed way).

The following quote from Christina Cahill, in her introduction to the Sports Council (Northern Region) Performance and Excellence document, illustrates how, as often seems to happen in sport, partnerships and these three areas of Communication, Cooperation and Coordination often just happen – but we only hear when it does happen – what happens when the bits don't come together, how many people/ areas of sport are left uncatered for?

> *Just as we are dependent on a variety of organs and support systems to enjoy full health, a sports performer is reliant on several factors and areas of support to reach their full potential. It may appear as if some are more crucial than others but unless they are all available and working together the end results will not be as high.*

Why bother with partnerships; although simple, they can be extremely powerful. If we can lay ground rules from the start and share roles and responsibilities in a structured way playing to each of the partner's strengths, we can achieve real success. This is simply about identifying **clear** roles from day one for each partner. Most partnerships break down because of lack of clarity on who should be doing what.

I intend to look at two examples of partnership schemes in sports development. The first, the Nottinghamshire Sports Training Scheme (NSTS), was one in which partnerships, and the need for them, was something that evolved. A great concept when it was dreamt up, but how much more powerful it could have been had it identified **clear** roles for all the partners instead of one agency dominating.

In the initial aims and objectives for the NSTS, devised in 1988 and listed below, there is no mention of partnerships or working together to:

- create a county wide network that will serve to introduce young people to sport
- create a scheme whereby interest and involvement in sport can be stimulated
- create a system whereby talent can be identified and developed through a pyramid of performance
- assist in the creation of a system whereby youngsters who drop out of the scheme at any level are able to continue playing their chosen sport or take up an alternative.

After about 18 months of scheme activity, progress was reviewed and a long look was taken at what was happening in the scheme in relation to what was going on in work at other agencies. The results were quite startling – there were no real links with education, governing bodies, clubs, etc. As a result of this, and of the biggest fear that youngsters were dropping out, the PENS Project (Performance and Excellence in Nottinghamshire Sport) was devised with the following aims and objectives:

- To review structures of governing bodies involved in NSTS assessing Performance and Excellence programmes as they relate to junior development.
- To establish, in liaison with governing bodies of sport, **new** programmes feeding into junior county squads and high level clubs.
- To establish programmes to assist participants and parents in the transition from structured sessional coaching into squad and club programmes.
- To investigate support services in liaison with relevant agencies.

The clear message running through these objectives is partnership. Coaching is one area in which real working partnerships are now beginning to evolve. One example of this is the production of a coaching review document – a partnership between the County Council, District Councils, County governing bodies of sport and sports clubs. Links with County governing bodies to employ coaching coordinators on annual honorariums, links with governing bodies and clubs to establish a County Coaches forum and annual conference, and the start of talks with education on developing the role of coaches in after-school sport.

The second example is one which hinged everything it had on partnerships. When Champion Coaching came into Nottinghamshire in 1991, two major initiatives occurred:

- It enabled a new route to be found into PE to look at ways in which education and Champion Coaching could work together.
- It brought County governing bodies and schools associations together.

Champion Coaching relies on the power of partnerships and is working hard to encourage partnerships at a local level – not an easy thing to do, but it does become easier if we can identify clear roles for each partner, and if we can find a tool which brings them together.

Champion Coaching learnt two major lessons from its pilot stage:

- To expand numbers there had to be an increase in the number of local coaches qualified and interested in working with children.
- To be sustainable, Champion Coaching must offer its activity in a coordinated community structure.

These lessons must now be the focus for our development of partnerships if we are to move things forward.

Champion Coaching has a mission –

> *To promote quality assured youth sport coaching for performance*
> *motivated children within a coordinated community structure*

and has identified five major partners who need to work together to achieve it:

- The Sports Councils.
- Delivery partners (typically local authorities).
- Governing Bodies of Sport.
- Physical Education.
- The National Coaching Foundation.

If these five networks are all to work together to one mission it is crucial that they are clear about the environment in which they are working (how often do we give our partners this?) The environment we are working in is out of school sport:

- The provision for out of school sport varies in quantity and quality.
- Many existing networks have an interest in delivering after school sports.
- Putting partnerships into practise is difficult.
- National coordination works for consistent effective delivery for children.

In attempting to develop quality and clear roles and responsibilities, Champion Coaching has a blueprint. These are simple steps which we need to go through and for each of which we need to identify a lead:

- The identification and briefing of a youth sport manager to act as a link between the local community and the National Coaching Foundation.
- The establishment of a youth sport advisory group.
- The undertaking of a local community audit – coaches, facilities, exit routes, existing provision.
- School/teacher liaison.
- Selection of sports.
- Development of exit routes for youngsters and coaches.
- Draft of budget.
- Recruitment and training of coaches.
- Nomination and assessment of children.
- Schedule of sport programmes and resource packages.
- Delivery of sport programmes.

If partnerships are really to work, all partners must be clear on why they are being involved and what they are all working towards. Get them to ask themselves the following questions:

- Why are they involved?
- Who should be involved from within their organisation?
- What involvement do they want?
- Where does their involvement fit in with their aims and objectives?
- How will they be involved?

Once this has been agreed, partners have to find a way of regular communication to ensure that we get our quality and achieve our mission (essentially this is a check on roles), and also that we get the right people to the right place at the right time for the right reasons.

An example of this communication in Champion Coaching is in the establishment of a local youth sport advisory group, made up of the key agents in the partnership. This group is responsible for the local decision making and makes partners accountable to one another.

If we can think around all of this we should be able to make partnerships easier, and in so doing, make good quality delivery for our kids (our future). So where is the concept of partnerships going?

I believe there are four key areas to be addressed:

- Quality v Quantity.
- Organisation v Fragmentation.
- Coordination and Communication.
- Planning for Partnership.

The last is especially vital. If we do not plan for our partnerships, they will never be easy.

# A Place For Everyone

## Alan Launder

*Alan Launder is Senior Lecturer at the School of Physical Education, University of South Australia. His major professional interests lie in the area of teacher education in physical education. Since 1984 he has been Field Events Coach to the Australian Olympic Team.*

Sport can provide wonderful opportunities for self fulfilment as well as a valuable tool for education. How many coaches can remember those marvellous moments when they experienced fantastic feelings of achievement? More important, how many can remember the seemingly insignificant things which were part of their early experiences? Looking fearfully out of the window at gathering clouds which could mean that a game would be cancelled; the ritual of inspecting the pitch in a cricket match; checking the notice board to see if you had been drawn in the same heat as the star runner; seeing your name in the team for the first time, carrying the cricket bag every step of the way from station to ground and back again; seeing the dew on the pitch and knowing passing the ball would be easy; all these and many more I can recall as if they were yesterday.

It is vital for coaches to drag back their memories of those early days in sport and remind themselves of the innocent joy they experienced then. Unfortunately, too many children go through life without ever experiencing those marvellous feelings of joy and satisfaction which can come merely through involvement – not merely success in sport.

This is why I must argue that the key to sport for all lies with the committed and skilful physical education teacher. Children will not, or at least only rarely, have the confidence to approach a sports club if they have never been previously exposed to the activity concerned. Children are as much worried about the prospect of the agony of defeat and failure as they are thrilled by the prospect of victory and success. Many would rather not try at all than risk the perceived embarrassment associated with incompetence. Only the sensitive teacher who has gained their trust can induce beginners to take their first uncertain steps towards mastery. In many ways the role of the coach and that of the teacher are very similar. However the differences can be crucial, for while the coach is inevitably goal directed and sees the child as a potential 'performer' in 'their' sport, the good teacher sees the child as just that, a child. Only the teacher who provides a whole range of activities for children to try and who helps them towards mastery of those activities is in a position to suggest that a commitment to one or the other might be best for any particular child.

My experience suggests that there is far more sporting talent in any school or community than any single coach could see. Much of that talent is hidden and it takes both patience and time for it to emerge. Attempts to identify the talented child early will rarely succeed, in fact they will usually flounder when the precocious youngster begins to mark time and the latent talent of others has been ignored or unseen. By creating a positive attitude to taking part, not towards succeeding let alone winning, many children who would otherwise be overwhelmed by the anxiety of possible failure will come forward to have a go. De Coubertin was absolutely right with his priorities, and sporting organisations which ignore them do so at their peril.

Having stressed the importance of the physical education teacher it is now time to add that the more 'coaches' there are in a community, the greater likelihood there is of a strong sporting culture evolving. While coaching at the highest level is a very complex task demanding a vast range of knowledge and skill, sports must be prepared to accept and encourage anyone willing to provide leadership. Parents must be involved as much as possible for while the parent on the outside can often be a real nuisance, in a coaching role they can be very valuable. However, if this is to work, sport must generate working models of instruction and of coaching such as 'the Ps of perfect pedagogy' developed in Australia so that novices have some basis to start with. This particular teaching model was developed for use by novice teachers but could easily be adapted for coaching in any sport.

## The Ps of Perfect Pedagogy – A Working Model of Instruction

| | |
|---|---|
| Pre-test | To determine where the learners are. |
| Planning | The best possible learning situation to attain predetermined worthwhile objectives. |
| Preparation | Of the learning environment to ensure that it is safe and conducive to learning: it may involve selection of an appropriate practice area.<br>Of the student for the learning experience. The instructor can affect the critical 'set to learn' by presenting an image of enthusiasm, confidence and commitment to the activity involved. |
| Presentation | Of the motor plan, problem or task so that the learner has a clear picture of what and how to practice. |
| Providing Plenty of Perfect Positive Practice | Learning is done by the learner and not by some kind of transmission process from the teacher. It is best achieved when the learner meets an appropriate challenge and masters the task after experiencing early success. |

**Which is:**

| | |
|---|---|
| Protected | The primary responsibility of the instructor is to ensure a safe learning situation. |
| Purposeful | Structured so as to ensure that the learner is motivated to concentrate hard on achieving mastery. |
| Persistent | Structured so that the learner is motivated to strive for success even when mastery is delayed. |
| Pertinent | Only practice which is appropriate to the level of the learner and the nature of the activity is of value. |
| Progressive | The level and nature of the challenge must be continually modified to match the progress of the learner. |
| Paced | To ensure that the learner is not bored by inactivity nor overwhelmed by continuous hard effort. |
| Personalised | So that individuals are challenged at their own level. |

| Playful | Without the play-like quality which underpins all sport much of the effort will be wasted. |
| Praise | To help learners feel good about themselves, the activity and the instructor. |
| Positioning | Of the class and the teacher to ensure safety, positive reinforcement and – |
| Perception | To be able to see what is actually happening, to be 'with it' and as a basis for – |
| PHeedback | Although this should be built into the task where possible, feedback must also be provided by the teacher. |
| PHlexibility | The ability to adjust quickly to changing circumstances is a critical one for the teacher/coach. However it is a difficult skill and is usually only developed with experience. |

All with *poise, patience* and *empathy* to lead to *positive participation* in the *future*.

| Post test | To discover what has been learned. |

While school physical education programmes are critical and the contribution of parents potentially important, government at all levels must be involved to bridge the gap between school, family and the community. The South Australian model of junior sport development (see below) might provide a useful model for Britain, for it is attempting to draw together the work of schools, clubs, sporting bodies and community agencies interested in the promotion of health to provide a coherent programme which will broaden the basis of participation at all levels. One aspect of this programme which could easily be copied is the use of high school students as sports leaders in primary schools. Not only would this provide some leadership for primary level programmes but may also bring many children into coaching.

### The Major Objective of the Junior Sports Policy

*To provide the best possible sporting experiences for all children with the view to encouraging life long, successful, active participation in sport. That participation focuses on enjoyment and on self esteem.*

The critical question which must be faced by all thinking people is 'what kind of a society do we wish to live in?' The American example is surely not one to emulate. While elite professional sport in that country provides a few with great wealth and many business opportunities for promotion, their society appears to be crumbling. While it would be going too far to argue that a broader range of sporting opportunities for all would rapidly change the situation, it would do no harm. Certainly when most western societies are facing a crisis in dealing with their youth in terms of suicide, drug abuse, crime and vandalism, solutions must be found. Sport is one area in which young people can be successful, and at a time in their lives when they cannot be perceived to be successful in any other field. For some it will provide them with the only positive experiences they may have in their whole life – a sobering thought indeed.

# Coaching the Elite

## Alan Launder

The data sheet for track and field confirms the importance of finding the very talented athlete in the 14 to 18 age group. The critical period may vary for other sports but with the expectations of gymnastics and swimming it is likely to be in this range.

Every coach must consider the place of their sports in a particular society and understand the way in which elements of this particular society impact on their role. Track and field in Australia, for example, is a coach driven sport; there is no support from the media and because of the geography and demography of the country the competition structure is weak. This means that the role of the track and field coach in Australia differs in many respects from that of the British coach where the sport is driven by its competition structure and media support, or Finland, where one could argue that the sport is culturally driven.

Only by understanding these factors is a coach able to appreciate the problems they are likely to face in both attracting and retaining talented youngsters and creating the support structures necessary to ensure that their talent is fully developed. Thus, while the role of the coach in any sport is difficult and complex, some sports have a decided advantage because of cultural factors; for example, soccer in the UK and basketball in the USA. In both cases recruiting youngsters into the sport is almost a non issue: compare this with the problem a volleyball coach or a field hockey coach might face in an inner city area in either country.

Thus for many coaches talent search or 'diamond mining' becomes a critical part of their role. Here I can only commend the approach developed by the East German rowing coaches and presently being applied with considerable success in South Australia. The rowing coaches at the South Australian Sports Institute have applied the unsophisticated methods of the DDR and are finding very talented youngsters, who remarkably have in many cases not been involved in any other competitive sport. The methods involved are quite simple and could be obtained from any rowing coach in the UK.

Here it must be stressed very often the critical factor which will determine success is not obvious physical ability but a steely determination to be the best – which is not always immediately obvious but only emerges when the grind of committed training begins. This means that coaches must throw their vision very wide in the first instance and follow a policy of accepting rather than rejecting youngsters.

Once the diamond has been found it must be carefully assessed to determine its final form. This means that coaches must be aware that a youngster's real talent may not lie in the event or even the sport they coach and should be prepared to let them go where they will do best. This is not easy, but in the long run is clearly the right thing to do; certainly a willingness to do this would do much to raise standards in many sports in the UK.

Now the diamond must be cut and polished. The Australian Institute of Sport and the various state institutes were established to ensure:

- good coaching
- training facilities
- equipment
- sports science support
- sports medicine support
- appropriate national and international competition
- assistance with finding work and developing a career plan
- assistance in gaining admission to suitable academic courses
- stipends to permit essential training time
- financial assistance to meet costs of massage, sauna, etc.

An indication of the level of planning involved in the sports science/medicine area of SASI, for example, is provided by the following materials.

Clearly the coach of talented youngsters becomes a manager and must be able to use all the support structures effectively. In many ways this broadens the demands on the coaching role, because it becomes essential to develop at least a working knowledge of many of the above areas to be able to communicate with the 'experts'.

Finally, the coach working with youngsters, talented or otherwise, must have a clear philosophy, for without this talent development becomes merely a 'meat market'. Coaches have the potential to make a huge contribution to any society as they help young people grow. I would hate to think that in a hundred years from now the sports sociologists of that time will look upon today's coaches as merely an extension of a long line of 'trainers' which began with the gladiatorial spectacles of Rome!

# Games for Excitement

## Alan Launder

Games are a valuable part of the educational process, but despite their great popularity, the major games of the world are often badly taught. Traditional approaches to teaching games have followed three distinct patterns. The coaching approach focuses on the development of the so-called fundamentals of basic skills or techniques such as kicking, controlling, heading and dribbling, for example in soccer. Unfortunately this approach often leaves children with little understanding of the fundamental nature of the game or even of the primary rules, so that they are ill prepared to play the game when it is offered to them.

The minor games approach provides lots of 'fun' but does little to help beginners learn the techniques, tactics or rules of the game because the only connection between the two is often in the name such as 'soccer rounders', and the fact that a soccer ball is used. The final, perhaps most cynical, approach employed by lazy or incompetent teachers is 'let's play the game', where teams are picked and the children thrown into a full game straight away. Here play is dominated by the more aggressive or experienced children while those with limited ability hover on the fringes trying to make sense of the apparently chaotic whirl of play going on around them.

We believe that if we are to give all children a chance to experience feelings of satisfaction and achievement when playing games, then we must employ an approach based around 'Mini games' which are reduced and sometimes slightly modified versions of the 'real game'. The scale of the game and the degree of modification will depend on the level of the students and the objectives of the teacher. Five vs five soccer played on a small pitch is an excellent example of a good mini game, for it provides far more opportunities for all children to really be involved and is also an excellent lead up to the full game. Because children like to play the full game, it may be necessary to explain the advantages of mini games in terms of the greater opportunities there are for every child to actively participate. It may also be worthwhile showing a video replay of a game and pointing out that when the camera zooms in to focus on play around the ball, it tends to show what is in effect a mini game with only a limited number of players involved.

In addition to ensuring more individual participation the teacher can focus practice on the development of specific techniques, tactics or skill by varying the dimensions of the playing area, changing the ways in which 'goals' can be scored or even by applying particular 'conditions' to the game. In this way five vs five soccer is a 'working model' of the real game and a learning laboratory for it. Three vs three half court basketball is another obvious example of an excellent mini game which can be used by the skilful teacher to achieve a wide range of outcomes.

A simple mini game for American football is played as follows: On a playing area 120' by 45', three attackers O face two defenders X. The attacking team has four downs to score a touchdown or advance the ball as far as possible downfield. The centre O1 snaps the ball to the quarterback O2 and then sets off with wide receiver O3 to run a pass pattern. The two defenders try to intercept or break up the play. In this first simple mini game no running with the ball is allowed and neither the quarterback nor the defenders are allowed to move over the line of scrimmage, so that only a passing game is played. To make the quarterback's task even easier in this first game they are allowed as long as they need to throw the pass. The third defender O3 acts as an official for one play and then rotates into the game for O1 who becomes the new official. Obviously it is possible to progress rapidly to include running plays and defensive responses.

Baseball and softball can all be played in mini form, though with far more modification than is required in the examples given above. Three batters take turns to have three hits – each from a tee if necessary – into a sector which represents the extended triangle, home plate, second base and third base. The sector is marked out with cones at suitable distances, say 60 feet, so that the batter can drive in 1, 2, 3 or 4 runs on each of three at bats. When the first inning is completed the batters and fielders change over roles and the new batting team tries to score more runs than their opponents.

In these games teachers can create their own rules. For example if you wish to penalise players who hit long balls and are caught, you simply deduct five runs from the batting team's score for every catch. One simple way of developing the game is to have the sector based around home plate, first and second. Now the batter has to hit and run; if they get to first safely, the runs they batted in are scored, if not they are lost. At the next level they have to get to second base to score their runs. Clearly these mini games will have a positive impact on the development of valuable fielding skills while also being great fun. The perceptive teacher will quickly add additional enjoyment by commenting on great plays and particularly by looking for the catch or play of the day.

Mini games in all their forms can also be structured to achieve specific objectives by simply varying the attacker/defender ratio and giving the numerical advantage to one or the other. Four vs one, three vs one, five vs two, three vs two and four vs three ratios represent a gradual progression for children as their passing skills and tactical awareness improve through a unit of soccer. On the other hand two vs three or two vs four games might be used to help top class players learn how to deal with the problems faced by outnumbered attackers at the highest levels of the game.

In basketball, three vs one and three vs two transition games are excellent mini games which will motivate children to 'play practice' purposefully for long periods. Similar games have been developed for the teaching of a whole range of other major sports. It should be pointed out that children have always used small sided games in their own informal games. While this is often because there are not enough players for the full game, it is also done to reduce the amount of running required and to focus on the most enjoyable elements of the game.

Even in their simplest form, mini games of this kind ensure that most, if not all, children are actively involved in both playing and learning. Because of this we have coined the phrase 'play practice' to emphasise the fact that games used in this way are legitimate learning situations. The teacher does not simply set up mini games and let them run without any intervention, hoping that desired outcomes will result. They must teach through these games using well timed breaks and 'freeze replays' to help players better understand what is required and to ensure later transfer to the full game. A 'freeze replay' is a simple teaching device; at a precise moment the teacher freezes play with a whistle blast and then moves players backwards and forwards slowly just as television does to highlight what happened, to introduce new concepts or to use a problem solving approach to help students work out other possible responses to the situation involved.

To use mini games even more effectively as play practice situations, teachers can 'condition' them to emphasise the specific technical or tactical aspects of a game. This method has been employed by soccer coaches for many years and experience has shown it can be used in the teaching of a wide range of games. For example, if the condition is that players in a soccer mini game are allowed only two touches of the ball at any one time, dribbling is immediately curtailed and passing will be encouraged. As the game continues other elements of good play can be developed. Players will quickly begin to be more precise with their first controlling touch and also more aware of potential receivers even as they move to take the ball. Gradually all players will become more conscious of the need to move into good positions to support each new receiver and to use good clear calls such as 'man on', 'hold on', 'turn' or time so that the ball player is made aware of how much space and thus time they have.

It is clear that well timed progression is important to ensure that the children are continually being challenged to move on to higher levels of play. It is also important that the condition applied is not artificial but rather encourages an aspect of the game that participants can see needs to be improved if they are to play better. For example, if a three vs three half court game of basketball is conditioned so that the ballhandler can only score by their own efforts with no screens or give and go moves, we would quickly see an improvement in their ability to operate from the triple threat position, combining outside shooting with fake and drive moves for the lay up or the pull up jump shot. However, this condition will set the scene for a whole range of technical and tactical development when used by a knowledgeable teacher.

Beginning with the simple one vs one condition this mini game will lead in an almost precise sequence to the improvement of one on one defensive skill, then defensive help, offensive spread and balance, penetrate and pitch out moves, defensive recovery by the helping defender, drive and dish moves and so on. Eventually a whole range of skilled play in basketball will have been explored and developed.

Teachers might also wish to consider the way in which a simple modification of the 'goal' can have enormous implications for the tactics used in a mini game. For example if we use extra large (60') goals in a soccer mini game we will encourage players to look for goal and shoot from much further away, while if we use very small goals (6') we will force attackers to interpass or dribble for a good close shot. We would also find defenders putting more pressure on the ball player in the first game and tending to use a zonal defence in the second.

Another simple modification which can be used to achieve more purposeful and pertinent play is the use of differential scoring. Most teachers would be aware of the significant impact the 'three point' shot has had on basketball, but few may be aware of the way this concept can be used in the teaching of games. For example, if a teacher is using a one on one practice to teach both attacking and defending moves, they will quickly find the practice breaking down because of the relative inability of the attacker to shoot from the outside. In the same way that defenders at the highest level drop off the poor outside shooter to protect against the drive to the basket, so will the novice defender play the outside shot passively and do everything to stop the drive.

However, if the teacher sets up a one vs one tournament where the results are recorded and introduces the differential scoring system, young players will quickly begin to play honest defence so that the opportunities for the attacker to learn the required offensive moves are improved. In this case, differential scoring simply involves giving the regular two points for a scored lay up **but** five points if the attacker hits the rim with their outside shot and ten if they manage to score over the defender. While such artificial devices may not be necessary in the USA they are in other countries, and perhaps this example illustrates the general concept.

By manipulating the number and balance of players, the playing area, the equipment used, the demands of the task, how goals or runs are scored it is possible to create a vast range of mini games which will give more children a chance to participate actively, to enjoy playing and to improve their understanding and skill as they do so. However, by controlling one more variable, that of **time,** it is possible to further heighten the games experience for children. Time as a variable seems to have attracted little interest from those writing about the teaching of games. Even a cursory glance at the contemporary sporting scene will clearly show that there are critical periods, usually but not always at the end of the game, when time seems to stand still, seconds become hours and when players commit everything as they strive for victory. These magic moments are more and more being captured on videotape for the continued vicarious enjoyment of millions of fans.

By limiting the playing time of a mini game to between three and five minutes we can keep the scoreline close and ensure that the play practice is both urgent and purposeful. Every move counts, every score is important and every mistake costly so that children can begin to experience feelings of participation and achievement even if it is only in a physical education lesson.

When mini time games are made part of a fantasy World Championships, Olympic games or World series, with results recorded on a championship table and with trophies for the best team, most sportsmanlike, best defence, best offence, most determined etc. then you will really see youngsters committed to purposeful play.

There are two other issues to be addressed in the teaching of games. Children like to play games, they like being challenged but they like to succeed. They do not want to fail and they certainly do not want to be overwhelmed or humiliated by their opponent. While the mini game approach will go a long way to resolving this problem, teachers must be aware that many children are more concerned about 'the agony of defeat' than striving for 'the thrill of victory'. Teachers must therefore continually stress that victory and defeat are just two sides of the same coin and that both are irrelevant to the more important process of participation. Children will appreciate and enjoy games more if they accept this idea; it may even be worth presenting the Olympic motto in every games unit.

Even though our students have had great success with this play practice approach based on small sided games they still find themselves facing problems dealing with resistant learners. Most children love to play games but they only make a complete commitment for as long as the game seems fair and the result stays in doubt. This of course is not unusual in adult play, even with highly paid professional players. Children certainly do not like being beaten. So, to ensure that children 'play practice' purposefully, indeed, with absolute commitment, the game score must be kept as close as possible and the chance of personal failure or embarrassment reduced.

It is clear that teachers must have a coherent personal philosophy of sport if they are to help children deal with the problems of participation. Unfortunately no philosophy, even one completely in tune with the thinking of modern sports psychology, will sustain children who are being thrashed in a game, particularly if personalities are involved. It was from the struggle to find solutions to these problems that the innovative concept of 'Fantasy games' evolved. The process was one of gradual evolution with ideas being drawn together from both theory and practice to produce tentative solutions which were then trialed and evaluated by student teachers in many different schools.

When the very first fantasy game was tried over ten years ago the teacher merely 'set the scene' verbally and let the players pretend they were playing matches in the World Table Tennis championships. Children were given a list of world class players whose names they could assume if they wished to. In the first fantasy game the score was set at 15-15 and the children simply played the game out. Depending on the final score of that game, for example 21-19 or 21-15 etc. they agreed on the starting score for the second game, eg. 15-16 or 15-18 and also decided who would serve first. In the third game the score was again adjusted and the match finished.

Even this simple approach to fantasy games generated higher levels of concentration and performance, particularly when combined with a tournament board where the results of the 'championships' were recorded. Because games always started at 15-15, every point was important when playing to 21 so that play tended to be very purposeful indeed. Other advantages quickly emerged; games between individuals took far less time than the full game and the scoreline could never be embarrassing because even the poorest player had at least 15 points to start with. What was most encouraging was the willingness of students to commit themselves to the 'fantasy' and play the games out seriously.

The next development was to produce and trial 'fantasy game' cards. The scene was set by the information on the card and the children could either choose which player they wanted to be or they could toss a coin to decide. In either case the match was played out as if it were a real championship. An additional benefit of using the cards was that the teacher was now 'free' to help individual children who might be experiencing difficulty.

Student teachers quickly discovered that the 'action fantasy game' concept could be used to deal with some of the major problems of teaching a game such as tennis where the children are often dispersed over a large area and where there is usually a wide range of ability. In fact, the true potential of this approach began to emerge when a student teacher had to use tennis courts in three different areas of a school in order to maximise individual participation in their lessons. By trying a range of strategies and in particular fantasy game cards, she was able to manage this difficult situation and to ensure that worthwhile learning occurred.

Student teachers also found that it was often the more experienced players who quickly lost interest and practiced or played very casually. Their careless attitude rubbed off on classmates nearby so that the quality of work from the whole class quickly deteriorated. One solution was to use the better players as assistant teachers, but even this was not appropriate for long periods as the teacher clearly had a responsibility to improve their play as well.

The best solution to this problem was to make up a series of 'fantasy game' cards based on great players playing in major tournaments as shown in the accompanying examples. At the beginning of the lesson, students paired up and selected a fantasy game card randomly from a box of such cards. After deciding 'who' they were, they played out the game.

The next step was to put a brief but specific 'practice task' on the reverse side of each card which had to be completed before the match could begin. To maintain the fantasy element these practice tasks were set up as either 'the match warm up' or as 'practice just prior to a restart after a rain delay', 'an injury' or even 'a bomb scare'. In the most recent development of this concept the practice cards require the players 'to hit forehand drives like Lendl or Steffi', or 'to keep the ball in play like Martina or Agassi'. To continue the developmental notion some cards also carried information about the way that player executed a particular stroke.

The cards themselves have taken many different forms but thick paper or stiff card of approximately 8" x 4" has been found to be most satisfactory. Cards of different colours can be used for different sexes or to distinguish cards for doubles, for example. Where possible the cards should be laminated to help them withstand the inevitable wear and tear and they should be kept in a box clearly labelled for a particular sport. Ideally they should also have colour photographs of the players or teams involved on them.

The fantasy games concept has been used extensively across the whole range of sports played in Australia, which in fact would appear to take in most of the games played around the world. They have been combined with the use of mini games to create cameo situations where young players commit themselves fully as they become immersed in the fantasy. The matches chosen and the game situations highlighted can involve teams at any level from local leagues, through National leagues, World series, Test matches, World championships and the Olympic games. The scenario established can be set in the future or it can recreate critical situations or periods from famous games of the past. In many ways these short fantasy games are very much like the simulations which good coaches use to prepare their players for those same critical periods or situations which can occur in any game.

One of the interesting things which was noticed when fantasy games were used was that the students actually began to take on the persona of the players concerned. As a result they were able to accept a lost game more cheerfully because they were not 'personally' involved, so that games between individuals were played in a much better spirit than would usually be the case. There were, however, occasions when teams of boys became so involved in the 'competition' that examples of bad sportsmanship surfaced. While this can be seen as a negative aspect of the fantasy game approach it also provided the teachers involved with opportunities to deal with issues of critical importance to the field of Physical Education.

Fantasy games have been used for many years now by young teachers in South Australia to encourage students to 'play practice' purposefully even when they are not directly supervised. There are several additional advantages. The use of fantasy games at the beginning of a lesson encourages children to get ready quickly; even here the cards can be used in a very flexible way once the students are used to them. For example, the children must take the cards from the appropriate box on a random basis; if when the card is taken the fantasy game is facing them they can immediately begin the game. However, if a practice task is facing them they must complete the practice task before they can start the game. The chance element involved makes this approach very acceptable to children and they respond well to it. In addition, fantasy games encourage children to begin practising quickly and purposefully so that the teacher is 'free' to deal with the inevitable personal problems and minor organisational matters which occur at the start of any lesson.

The cards can also be used flexibly during a lesson to keep the better players on task, as a reward for students who have worked particularly well at a practice task, or to free the teacher to assist students in difficulty. The fantasy game concept is still evolving and developing in many creative ways and not always in the area of ball games, as the example below confirms.

An Adelaide student teacher, Sam White, applied it to a unit of work on cycling with excellent results. In this unit Sam was required to deal with the maintenance of cycles and safe highway riding. To encourage purposeful and careful riding habits as well as to ensure perfectly maintained cycles he created 'The Tour de West Lakes' which was the name of the area around his school. Sam modelled his 'race' on the world renowned Tour de France and brought to the school as much information as he could find about this great sporting event.

Each lesson included a ride of several miles which made up a 'stage' of the race. To eliminate racing and its attendant dangers Sam used the beautifully simple device of determining the finishing position and time **randomly**. As the riders finished each stage they picked a card from a box which allocated a 'position and riding time' so that the first student to finish might well draw a card which placed them last. This arrangement makes racing pointless and when combined with a system of time penalties for traffic offences or careless riding it ensured that the students rode sensibly and safely. Naturally he also had a time bonus system for all bicycles which were well maintained.

There were prizes for stage winners and the race leader, as in the Tour de France, wore the famed yellow jersey. There were special sections for 'sprints' and 'hill climbs' as in the real tour even though there was not a hill of any kind within 15 miles of the school. Stage results were published and there was a well organised presentation of prizes at the end of the race. While there is no research evidence to support this, we believe that few of the children involved will quickly forget this experience.

In a sense this article becomes a memorial for Sam who was tragically killed while on his cycle preparing for a Triathlon.

Finally, in any physical education experience, teachers should try to harness the intense feelings of pleasure and satisfaction when a movement task is well done. The sweet feeling of clean contact when a ball is properly hit, of mastery when it is controlled or caught, of satisfaction when intelligent team work produces a goal or thoughtful defence snares an interception, must all be highlighted and savoured. These are the magical moments which children can remember long after the result is forgotten and they, more than any other factor, are the reason why we continue to play even when our bodies can no longer sustain our dreams.

# Windows of Opportunity

## Brad McStravick

*Brad McStravick is a BAF National Coach in Athletics with national responsibility for school age athletes. He took up this position in July 1988, prior to which he worked for the BAAB as Schools Athletics Project Manager. He competed in two Summer Olympic Games in the Decathlon, and a winter Olympics in Bobsleigh, in addition to the other major championships. He was Team Coach to Great Britain at the 1988 Olympic Games, and is currently Chief Coach to the England Athletics Team.*

Traditionally, the assumption has been made that, one way or another, children are introduced to the sport of athletics at school. More than this, it has been assumed that early competitive opportunity is afforded at school and that, for the majority of those athletes who will reach the higher echelons of national and international competition, the National Schools Championships are the normal testing ground. Indeed, these championships can be seen as a 'talent selection process' – from school through to county level, to national and for some, international level, ie. the Home Countries Schools U17 International Match (at Cross Country and Track and Field).

Of course most, if not all, of these athletes belong to athletic clubs; many athletes of school age join clubs who are not a part of this process and this is more often than not the outcome of the athlete's initiative.

So, for the years from 6-16, the active input of the Governing Body to the development of athletes is not substantial. Until recently, it was only when athletes were at the age for inclusion in GB Junior Teams (U20) that selected athletes were included in the National Junior Squad. This meant attending a weekend get-together; linking in with Senior National Squads; having performance monitored; competing for the National Junior Team in International matches, and, for an elite group, at European and World Junior Championships. Clearly, there is a service for athletes provided by the sport – but very little is done for athlete development.

Taking things a stage further, once out of the Junior age group, very few athletes are immediately ready for Senior competition. The next two years, post Junior – the Contender age group (U23) – are critical years in athlete development, but again the sport itself does little for these athletes.

With these points in mind, the BAF is at present establishing these three groups to operate together in the Junior Development Commission. The Junior Development Commission monitors this single process of athlete development from an athlete's introduction to the sport through to departure from the Contender age group. The BAF is then actively involved in Junior Athlete Development and brings the sport into a more positive role in recruitment and development of young athletes and in athletics provision for the three age groups:

- School Age Athlete Group – 8 yrs to 16 yrs
- Junior Age Group – 17 yrs to 19 yrs
- Contender Age Group – 20 yrs to 22 yrs

My presentation will deal with the elite within my national responsibility for the School Age Athlete Group.

## The Elite Athlete (14-18)

Many athletes present themselves annually at the National Schools Track and Field Championships, at under 15 and under 17 age groups, and compete with distinction. But experience tells us that it is not necessarily the winners who go on to compete at Junior and Senior International levels. Many athletes of this age excel, often due to early physical development or coaching from an early age, or both, and sometimes leave the sport when the rest catch up and they lose their 'star' status or their performance levels out. Sometimes, however, it is the result of over zealous parents or of injury, or it is the fault of coaches who are only concerned with short term results and do not take into account the very important aspect of the long term development of athletes. Nevertheless, these athletes should not be dismissed. All those who are selected to compete at their National Schools Championships are 'the elite'; this represents 2000 at the English Schools Athletics Championships, 400 at the Ulster Schools Athletics Championships, 1300 at the Scottish Schools Athletics Championships and 900 at the Welsh Schools Athletics Championships. All have ability and potential and have demonstrated that by achieving the required qualifying standard.

I now co-ordinate the ESAA Championships survey and this year I attempted to obtain the details of **all** athletes who compete, to include the athlete's coach and athletics club. In previous years, this information was collected but for only the top six placings. This represents a major move forward because now, through the Regional National Coaches and Regional Coaching Committees, these people can be personally invited to coaching clinics, Regional Elite Squads, Regional Youth Training days etc. where their ability/potential can be assessed and monitored. This liaison could then be extended so that the Regional National Coach or Regional Event Coaches could establish contact with their coach (if they have one), and create a new environment of support and advice for these young athletes. The next stage is to co-ordinate this same exercise in Northern Ireland, Scotland and Wales, and this will happen next year.

This process is especially relevant for the Under 17 age group, many of who leave school, change school, go out to work etc. In other words, they have a major upheaval in their lifestyle and may find it difficult to continue in the sport. A minority will move straight into the Junior Athlete Group if their performance is of high enough merit. The majority will be struggling to find the same degree of success when they move up an age group and so there is greater emphasis placed on this group in terms of Regional support. The younger age group are often a transient group who 'ebb and flow on the tide of success'. There is a much greater link between elite performers at U17 level and those going on to international representative honours.

## Summary

Junior athlete development is seen as a continuous process from School age to Contender (from 8-22 yrs). The National Schools Athletics Championships provide a talent selection process, a screening process whereby athletes with ability and potential are identified. These athletes are then personally invited, by letter, to attend Regional Youth Squad training days where greater contact and support can be offered, and all efforts are made to assist with their continued progress in the sport. As the numbers pyramid narrows towards the National elite at U20 level, so these athletes are involved with the National Junior Squad but are also at Regional level.

There is a common feeling in many sports that there are fewer youngsters coming from schools into clubs; if that feeling is accepted as a fact, then it is prudent to at least look after what is there at present.

## Athletics for the School Age Athlete

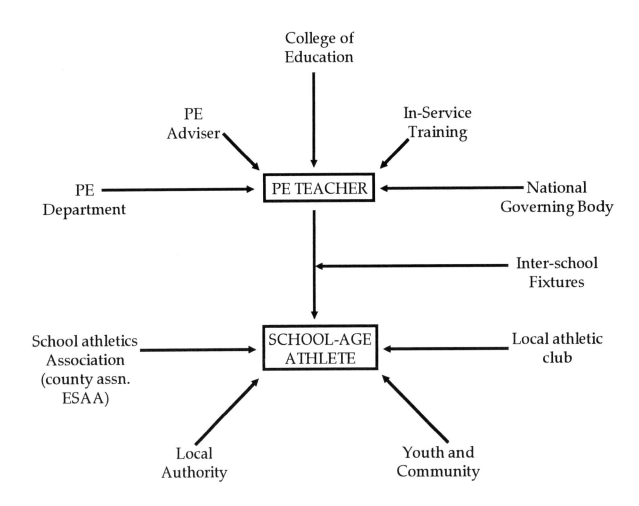

## Club Based Competition Opportunities

| Date | Type | Example |
|------|------|---------|
| Various | Open Meetings | Early indicators/fun |
| 1/5; 22/5; 12/6 2/7; 24/7; 11/8 | Local league meetings | West Yorkshire League |
| 21/4; 26/5; 30/6 28/7; 18/8; 1/9 | Area League meetings | South West League |
| 27/4; 11/5; 1/6 22/6; 20/7; 14/9 | Regional league | Southern Womens League |
| 28/4; 12/5; 2/6 23/6; 21/7; 7/9 | Regional/national leagues | Woolworths YA League |
| 6/5; 16/6; 28/7 25/8 | National league | UK Junior League |
| 18/19 May | County champs | Middlesex Champs |
| 15/16 June | Area champs | Northern Champs |
| 19/20 July | International match (U18) | Youth Olympic Games |
| 17/18 August | National champs (U17 & U15) | AAA/WAAA Champs |
| 15/6; 7/7; 14/7 20/7 | BAAB representative matches (U20) | GB vs USA; GB vs GER |
| 24 August | BAAB representative match (U19) | GB vs GER |
| 6-11 August | European/World Champs | Every year |
| Various | BAAB Senior representative matches | GB vs GER; GB vs URS |
| Various | Major championships | Olympic Games 1984 – Mafe European Champs 1990 – Smith, Richardson Europa Cup 1991 – Idowu |

**School Based Competition Opportunities**

| Date | Type | Example |
| --- | --- | --- |
| Various | Inter school | School sports day |
| May/June | Dual match | School vs school |
| 14/15 May | 10-12 schools match | District Champs |
| Various | Inter schools league | Herts Athletics League |
| 28 May | All schools | District Schools Champs |
| 30 May | ESAA Schools Cup | Regional Round |
| 8/9 June | Inter District Match | County Championships |
| 15 June | Inter County Match | Mason Trophy |
| 22/23 June | ESAA Multi Events | Regional Round |
| 6 July | ESAA Schools Cup | Finals |
| 12/13 July | National Schools | ESAA T & F Champs |
| 20 July | Home Countries Match (U17) | Eng vs Scot vs Ire vs Wales |
| 22/23 Sept | ESAA Champs | Walks & Multi Events |

**English Schools Athletic Association Finals 1992 – Athletes and Results**

| Surname: | 100m | | | Junior Boys | |
| Forename: | PB: | | | DOB: | |
| Address: | Perf | Std | Wind | Pos | Heat |

Post Code:

Telephone:                    Club:                              Coach:

| Surname: | 100m | | | Senior Boys | |
| Forename: | PB: | | | DOB: | |
| Address: | Perf | Std | Wind | Pos | Heat |

Post Code:

Telephone:                    Club:                              Coach:

| Surname: | 100m | | | Junior Girls | |
| Forename: | PB: | | | DOB: | |
| Address: | Perf | Std | Wind | Pos | Heat |

Post Code:

Telephone:                    Club:                              Coach:

| Surname: | 100m | | | Senior Girls | |
| Forename: | PB: | | | DOB: | |
| Address: | Perf | Std | Wind | Pos | Heat |

Post Code:

Telephone:                    Club:                              Coach:

**Where Are They Now? (Boys U15 – U17 – U19)**

| 1986 | 1988 | 1990 |
|---|---|---|
| Pole vault: | | |
| 1 MA Brunshill | 1 Hodgkinson (?) | 1 Belsham (–) |
| | 2 A Greig | 2 W Siley |
| | 3 W Siley | 3 M Grant (–) |
| | 4 M Brunshill (?) | 4 B Thomas (12) |
| | | 5 D Mellor (8) |
| Javelin: | | |
| 1 P Smith (?) | 1 Harrison (?) | 1 Wilkes (–) |
| | 2 A Smith (?) | 2 Medcroft (6) |
| | 3 Hinton | 3 Neiland (13) |
| Hurdles: | | |
| 1 R Fisher | 1 D Bainbridge | 1 M Stern |
| | 2 J Stevenson (–) | 2 J Quarry (TJ) |
| | 3 M Stern | 3 D Lewis (–) |
| High Jump: | | |
| 1 C Trimby (?) | 1 B Reilly | 1 B Reilly |
| | 2 S Smith | 2 S Smith |
| | 3 B Oakley (?) | 3 Skelding (?) |

**Where Are They Now? (Girls U15 – U17 – U19)**

| 1986 | 1988 | 1990 |
|---|---|---|
| High Jump: | | |
| 1 L Haggett | 1 L Haggett | 1 Smith (12) |
| | 2 Anderson (?) | 2 C Phythian (200m) |
| | 3 MacDonald | 3 A Purton (8) |
| | | 10 MacDonald |
| 100m: | | |
| 1 A Soper | 1 G McLeod | 1 A Soper |
| | 2 F Page (?) | 2 J Riley (4) |
| | 3 R Dunthorne (?) | 3 Lowdwell (5) |
| 200m: | | |
| 1 D Fraser | 1 D Fraser | 1 D Fraser |
| | 2 J Williams | 2 V Theobald (hurd) |
| | 3 S Baker | 3 M Richardson (4) |
| Long Jump: | | |
| 1 D Lewis | 1 D Lewis | 1 J Wise (100m 1st R) |
| | 2 J Harris | 2 Y Idowu (100m 1st R) |
| | 3 Y Hallet | 3 J McCoy (9) |

# Plans into Action

## Pat Nicholl

*Before Pat Nicholl joined the Sports Council (Southern Region) in 1983, she was a teacher for five years, followed by a short career commission in the Royal Navy with a varied range of appointments, including Staff Officer to a submarine and helicopter squadron. Since joining the Sports Council she has been able to develop her understanding, knowledge and interest in sport as a whole, and is currently Senior Regional Officer.*

During the next hour, I shall outline the Action Plan programme, and allow a short break for questions. We will then consider four of the general issues to emerge and this should leave enough time for discussion and a final summary.

I find it hard to believe that you have all volunteered to hear about plans and strategies. But I guess that, like me, you would rather talk about how we can just get on, get things done and make some progress, so I think we'll do that.

Let me take you back a bit to the dark age of 1989. Our team of six Regional Officers had been liaising as usual with probably about ninety of the sports that we recognised at that time. We attended lots of meetings and liaised very hard, and then we stopped to question the effectiveness of this approach.

Now without a doubt in all these sports many people were, and still are, doing a tremendous amount of work. But we felt that we were not making any difference.

- How could we find enough **time** to deal with key matters?
- How could we help bring about much needed changes?
- How could we strengthen these sports so that they could continue to make good progress on their own accounts?

In short, we devised the **Action Plan Programme.** It was and still is to some degree experimental. Indeed, most of our best work is through trial and error.

We took a new perspective and established these three principles:

- Just a few sports would receive special attention for a period of two years.
- A range of agencies would be drawn together to share their involvement in each sport.
- An agreed plan of action would form the basis for our work.

These plans are very simple – they take a view across the whole sport through a short series of issues, list priority areas and set a few recommendations for action.

Unfortunately, we have had to say 'no' to many other requests for help during this period, but we have always been keen to share relevant points of learning with the rest. Of the initial four sports; Netball has completed; Football, Tennis and Badminton are near completion with Hockey only commencing in June this year, (1992).

The Action Plan Programme has formed a key part of the **Regional Strategy** with its single aim, albeit a long one:

> *To assist and guide all sporting and recreational agencies in developing a practical framework for sport in the Region, so providing the opportunity for everyone to take part in sport as often and at whatever level they wish.*

We aim to work with sports organisations to develop a stronger structure for sport so that better, long-term opportunities are provided at all levels.

Some of you may not be used to learning from netball, but people from the South are well used to it by now. Using netball as the illustration, we covered the levels from Foundation to Excellence. Incorporated within the Netball Plan and Programme are elements such as schools netball, junior leagues, talent development programmes, netball centres, coaches associations and newsletters.

In August 1992 we produced the report, *Netball in the South*. Section One of the report covered the production and implementation of the plan, and the key achievements – Development Plans, Netball Centres, Talent Development Programmes, Links with Schools and Education, Information. Great success with much progress. As you can see, in this case:

- we have found time to deal with key matters
- we are helping bring about changes
- we are strengthening this sport so that they can continue to make good progress.

Sections Two and Three cover lessons learnt and prospects for the future.

*Netball in the South* is the first of our monitoring reports – football is being drafted, tennis and badminton will follow in the spring.

The lessons that are being learnt, whilst recorded within separate reports, will be drawn together and set into an Issues Paper which is due to be produced early next year. At this stage I would like to pause and ask if you have any questions about the Action Plan programme.

A great amount of effort has gone into the Programme and much has been achieved within the five sports. Whole areas such as Development Officers, Information and Communication, Facility Provision have been very much to the fore. However, I would like to return to some of the general points that are emerging that I feel will be of particular relevance to this audience.

### Roles and Responsibilities

The first is a difficult one, or we seem to find it particularly so.

A range of agencies such as school, local authorities, governing bodies, NCF, sports clubs, all make important contributions to any one sport. The difficulty we find is the uncertainty about who should be doing what, where we should be working together and where we can take quite separate responsibility.

The netballers have faced up to this challenge and set us a really good example through the recent South Region Netball Association (SRNA) development plan:

Some differences were identified:

- Youth Development.
- Performance & Excellence.
- Talent Development Programme.
- Schools.
- Saturday clubs.
- Junior League.

There were some common responsibilities, namely publicity and promotion, and some shared areas such as League and Local Authority in facility development.

Through clarifying and specifying in this way it should be possible to prevent wasteful duplication, to manage better the areas where we need to work together and to allocate at least one body to areas of neglect.

If we could get people to address their role and the role of their organisation, we feel we could make so much more of all their inputs. It makes working together so much easier.

### Pathways for Young Players

The second finding concerns young people.

The provision of pathways from introduction to highest level forms the framework of most Governing Body operations. The problem for many lies in attracting and maintaining the interest of young people.

Many of the speakers this weekend will deal with this subject, so I will just use the East Hants Badminton Project sheet to make a relatively small but important point.

There are a growing number of schemes like this. But I would ask you – how many are just short-term, like courses? Obviously these have a value in themselves, but how many provide future options and continuation in the sport for the long term?

We believe many more long-term regular playing opportunities need to be provided in most sports. All five Action Plan sports placed young people as the highest priority. There is still a great deal to be progressed if we are to create these pathways and networks through to the top.

**East Hampshire Badminton for School Aged Children Project**

1  Aims of the Project

- To provide after-school badminton opportunities for school aged children in East Hants.
- To provide quality coaching in a fun and learning environment.
- To sustain the interest of the children by developing a local league and competitive situations.
- To develop pathways of further opportunities to county development cells and local clubs.

2  Partners involved in the Project

This localised project will involve the unique collaboration between:

- East Hampshire District Council
- Mill Chase Community School
- Bohunt Community School
- Horndean Community School
- Petersfield School
- Alton Leisure Centre
- The Taro Leisure Centre
- Badminton Southern Region Coaching and Development Committee
- Hampshire Active Partners
- The Sports Council (Southern Region).

Together these partners can offer all the essential ingredients (facilities, coaching, equipment, publicity, general expertise and finance) which can make this project happen and meet the aims outlined in the first section.

3  The Project

Junior Club       At four of the venues outlined above, after school badminton opportunities will be introduced offering a mixture of fun and serious play, with coaching to encourage better technique and further progression in the sport.

Local League      In order to sustain the interest of the young children and develop their potential, a league can be organised between the respective venues.

Links with clubs  Local badminton clubs will be encouraged to get involved with the project and draw interested young players into the club structure.

4  Developing the Project

The co-operation between all the partners will provide a small network of regular 'playing centres'. Each will offer various options for continuation of the game.

## Coaching

The third point covers coaching. All the sports addressed coaching to some degree, but in each case we faced the same questions.

- Where are our coaches?
- What are they doing?

If we are to run courses, to provide information and support, to help make the best use of all our coaches, it is clear that we need to know where and what our coaches are doing.

Through the Programme and with the help of the NCC Development Officer, Phillippa Mole, we have helped all five GBs set up coaches registers. They are gathering information on their coaches, and are beginning to realise the benefits. We hope they will take on these registers and develop them under their own auspices.

In addition I should like to highlight the benefits that have been gained through the formation of Coaches Associations and production of newsletters such as *Football Focus* and *Goal Attack*. Coaches tell us how much they value communication and support through these means. With these Registers, Associations and Newsletters we are in such a better position to effect Coaching Development Programmes, I wonder how we managed without them?

## Co-ordination

The final point is perhaps for us the most important of all. Co-ordination of everyone's efforts has been called for through the years, yet it has been most difficult to achieve. We feel that responsibility for co-ordination must lie with one body and we suggest most strongly this should be the Governing Body for Sport. Whether they are in a position to meet this responsibility fully is another matter. We may have to assist and support in some areas. Nevertheless, we believe it is the only way for the long term development of sport in our region.

In spite of weaknesses, there are some good examples of Governing Bodies taking responsibility and co-ordinating the contributions of many.

If our work on the Action Plan Programme has taught us many lessons, it has also made us realise the significance of Governing Bodies of Sport and the need for their good management.

We need to help them **manage** better; in other words, to plan and, with and through others, to take effective action.

I shall finish on that note and look forward to hearing your views.

# Introduction to Athletics: An Innovative/Inspirational Approach to the Teaching of Athletics to Young People

## Wilf Paish

*Wilf Paish was National Athletics Coach from 1964 to 1980, and during that period he attended every Olympic, European and Commonwealth Games meeting. Since 1984 he has been a freelance Sports Consultant, and specialises in the scientific aspects of sport and in applying these principles to practical situations. He is a prolific writer and makes regular contributions to press, Radio and TV.*

When I was appointed as the Alcoa Coach in residence based in Perth, Western Australia, my brief was to examine carefully the coaching structure of the 'Little Athletics Association', which provides coaching and competition for the younger age groups, based at well established training centres scattered throughout the state. The organisation could be established as a model for any successful sports organisation, complete with efficient administration, secretarial back-up, sponsorship, publications, brochures etc., indeed all that makes for successful recruiting of both children and parents as helpers. The young children have a book with appropriate 'stickers' which indicate their levels of attainment at any stage during the season. These stickers are produced by an excellent computer functioned system.

An examination of the coaching structure indicated that while the coaches were willing, their ability to organise fairly large groups of young children into units that could accept coaching was obviously lacking. The same could be said of their knowledge of performance techniques and simple motivational skills, such as fun games and competitions.

In order to remedy the situation, I came up with the idea of a set of simple coaching cards, all colour coded and cross referenced, to cover the three recognised age groups; there were ten cards for each age group. Each card provided the coach with a planned training evening, comprising an introductory running game; a skill practice session covering a jumping event and a throwing event, together with a concluding running game. The coach is thus provided with a series of activities which children like, and which are easy to organise. A reference set of cards explains all the various activities to the coach. When the set of ten cards has been completed, the coach can then select items on a random basis which will provide enough different sessions to occupy the whole of the summer season. The cards are laminated and very well produced. The total number of cards including the reference explanatory set is eighty-five.

The cards were extremely well received and are still used as a reference source for coaches.

On my return to the UK, I introduced the cards to selected groups of primary school teachers, since it was obvious that with a degree of modification they have a place in our teaching of physical education. Once again the cards have been received with enthusiasm and used with a lot of success. By and large the primary teacher is not trained to have such a specific ability which is normally reserved for the specialist teacher of physical education. The cards can help considerably in helping primary teachers to gain this expertise.

Various problems face the primary school teacher with specific reference to Key Sgtages 1 and 2 of the National Curriculum. For example, many of them are in their late 40s-early 50s, and were trained over twenty years ago; it isn't always easy to accept enforced change. As I said earlier, they have not received specialist training and lack 'the tricks of the trade', and may also lack confidence in their own ability to demonstrate. These cards offer a series of simple, planned lessons which will save them time and increase their confidence. The cards provide the coach with a series of activities which children like, and which are easy to organise.

Currently the cards are with Tameside advisory physical education teachers, and will be produced at a later stage for use in this country.

# The Hampshire Experience: Case Study – Hampshire Active Partners Project

## Steve Poynton

*Steve Poynton is a General Inspector in Physical Education. He has been closely involved with the establishment of the Hampshire and Southern Region Sports Council's partnership project 'Active Partners'. This project is managed by the PE Inspectorate, but is attempting to move towards a unified provision of quality opportunitites for youngsters, combining the work of many agencies under the project's philosophy.*

### Introduction

What is the Active Partners Project?

- It is a joint funded project between Hampshire Education Authority via the Physical Education Inspectors, and the Southern Region Sports Council.

- It is about forming partnerships between any trusted agency that can provide good quality opportunities.

- Almost every youngster attends school and receives physical education lessons. The quality of that work is the key for the future. Investment in supporting schools is essential if we are to produce active, healthy and sporting youngsters.

- Equally important is the development of any pathway for youngsters into their community, which will increase their involvement in enjoyable physical activity.

- The potential partners are many and varied. The Sports Council, National Coaching Foundation, governing bodies of sport, recreation and leisure departments, local clubs and facilities are all increasingly aware of their potential role and responsibilities when working with young people.

- By promoting good quality partnerships, starting from the existing educational infrastructure (and its philosophy), youngsters can be helped to fully realise their aspirations and potential in the full community.

Today we will use examples from this and other projects to look at:

- successes and good practice in establishing 'partnerships'
- the issues and possibilities of working with education
- the issues related to managing 'partnerships'.

**Active Partners Project Aims**

- To improve the **quality of physical education** in Hampshire Schools and colleges as a foundation for the future.
- To promote and develop **pathways** for pupils to increase their participation in and out of school and gain help with individual or group performance, through enjoyment and understanding.
- To promote and develop **partnerships** between all those agencies who are active in any geographical area or activity.
- To provide a **structure** that is a continuous and progressive experience for pupils developing from the existing education infrastructure into their community and beyond, that can fully realise their aspirations and potential.

From its outset, the project has used a good practice model to inform all its developments. The following are the 'first principles' we like to work from.

Partnership opportunities should:

- reflect the **needs** and **priorities** of the young people concerned
- enhance and **complement the basic provision** all pupils are entitled to
- provide **quality controlled pathways** for young people from the school curriculum, to further opportunities in their community
- work within a **logical geographical area**
- start from an **audit** of the current situation
- build upon **existing networks** and support agencies, adding to the **support infrastructure**
- **identify gaps** in the provision and help bridge them
- draw together **trusted local agencies** and providers in a quality controlled way
- **be well managed**
- ensure a **common approach** is established, moving towards a common foundation of skills, knowledge and understanding for young people:
  - Participation with understanding.
  - Fair play.
  - Leadership.
- understand **legal** and **health and safety** requirements
- establish **youth sport advisory groups** whenever practicable
- become involved in **teacher-coach education**:
  - Inset.
  - Coach lists.
  - Local coaching structures (NCF model).
- support, reward and give status to the role of local Coordinator, Fixer or Manager of such partnerships.

Acting from these 'first principles' a great many projects and activities have developed, such as the following.

**Project Developments: The Primary Model**

**Example: Ringwood Netball**
- Feeder primary schools to their secondary school community facility.

**Inset**
- Inset course by a local teacher and a coach.

**Support**
- Parent coaching course.
- Project coordinator support in schools.
- National 'mini-games' trial.

**Resources**
- Equipment 'loan' system.
- New resource – mini post.

**Festival**
- Festival event.

**Exit**
- Centre of development project.

**Route**
- Not expensive.

**Project Developments: Secondary**

**Example: Champion Coaching**
**Status**
- It has a national dimension, direction and quality control.
- It has high status.

**Quality**
- It has high quality pupil opportunities.
- It has high quality coaching (Head Coach), facilities and parental involvement.

**Education to community**
- It is attempting to value the role of physical educationalists.
- It requires a pathway between support agencies and planned exit routes.

**Management**
- It is attempting to establish the role of a Youth Sport Manager.

*Discussion Question:* Is a unified or coordinated provision of opportunity for school age youngsters a realistic aim?

## Working With Schools

It is important for anyone working with school age pupils to fully understand the situation in schools and with Physical Education in the National Curriculum.

### PE and the National Curriculum

There are three useful documents:

- The Final Working Party Report (DES August 1991).
- The Statutory Orders themselves (April 1992).
- The non-statutory guidance (June 1992).

They:

- outline a progressive and balanced programme of work
- support good sport
- support a 'Partnership Model' for physical education and sport
- are underpinned by a sound rationale.

### Activities
- Athletic activity.
- Dance.
- Games:
  - invasion games
  - net-wall games
  - striking and fielding games.
- Gymnastics activities.
- Outdoor and adventurous activities.
- Swimming.

### Issues Related to Adults Other Than Teachers Working With Schools

- The school 'curriculum' consists of all those activities planned and managed by the school: curriculum time, extended or extra curricular activity.
- Headteachers and principals should only appoint those people who have the correct training and experience to teach their particular age of pupils and curriculum activities.
- These qualified professionals have a 'duty of care' regarding their pupils (*in loco parentis*). It cannot be delegated.
- Headteachers and teachers are charged with implementing the whole curriculum, including the preparation of schemes or work.
- There are police criminal record search procedures for adults working with any independence in schools.
- Levels of 'supervision' are different from good practice.

## Primary School Issues and Developments

| | | |
|---|---|---|
| • Curriculum pressure | vs | Professional behaviour. |
| • Funding and facilities | vs | Wanting the best for their pupils LMS Freedom. |
| • PE Awareness and inset | vs | Development plan 'readiness'. |
| • Perceptions of PE | vs | Response to the document eg. General requirements. |
| • Perceptions of sport | vs | Wanting opportunities for their pupils. Positive educational experience with help. |

## The Potential Role of 'Responsible' Adults in Primary Schools

- Trained and informed parents working alongside teachers.
- 'Coaches' working alongside teachers (target = pupil and teacher).
- More independent work **only** when the **person specific requirement and training** are met (extended curriculum).
- Area – cluster development plan uses of facilities and expertise, eg. Secondary Schools, Leisure Centre, the use of Trusted Partners.

## Secondary School Issues and Developments

- Improved awareness and recognition and the challenges set.
- Improved planning and management.
- Improved primary liaison and awareness.
- Great knowledge and expertise, eg. Sports Council projects.
   **But**
- Time is a very precious resource.
- Need to have their views valued.
- Need to see the relevance and benefits (for staff and pupils).
- Need to be active in the 'partnership' process.

## The Potential Role of Adults in Secondary Schools

- Coaches working alongside teachers.
- Coaches leading activities, teachers leading pupils.
- More independent extended activity work when the person specific requirements and training are met.
- Independent extended activity in the community, only when the person specific requirements and training are met.
- Junior section work.
- Within a unified structure.
- Area and community development plan activity, eg. schools of sport.

*Discussion Question:*  What are the implications of working directly with schools and their pupils for you?

## Managing Youth Sport Developments

### Potential roles
- The school or group of schools coordinator.
- The 'logical geographical area' manager.

### Key issues

- Multi-activity overview ⎱ Area development
  Multi-agency overview ⎰ plan
- Management and leadership.
- Time.
- Status.
- Resources.
- Job Security – professional development.

### Key questions
- Does a 'key worker' have this role at present?
- Do we understand the evidence of success?
- Do we hope rather than pay?
- Can we pay together?

*Discussion Question:*  Who could or should manage such developments?

### Conclusion: The Need To Change – An Educational Response

Developing and managing pathways from the school curriculum to wider community opportunities:

- involves a variety of trusted partners
- leads to a 'Partnership Plan'
- needs to be well managed
- needs to have its foundations in education
- should have a significant role for teachers, as one agent in the process. In particular the good middle manager.

# Developing Common Core Skills

## Brenda Read

*Since 1978 Brenda Read has been a Lecturer and Director for In-service Education and Training in the Department of Physical Education, Sports Science and Recreation Management at Loughborough University. She played Hockey for England, Midlands, Leicestershire and Oxfordshire, and Cricket for Midlands, Oxfordshire and Warwickshire, and is an Advanced Coach of the All England Womens' Hockey Association. Brenda has had numerous publications, and is currently involved in researching playground play in primary schools.*

In September 1992 a resource was published entitled *'Teaching Children to Play Games 5-11: A Resource for Primary Teachers'*. This was the outcome of a partnership between physical education and sport under the auspices of the British Council of Physical Education, funded by The Sports Council with the support of The National Coaching Foundation. Two consultants were appointed to work with nineteen national governing bodies of sport. Phyl Edwards worked with the striking/fielding family of games and I worked with net/wall and invasion games.

The resource, which extends to 300pp, is colour coded. The red sections provide information for teachers on the planning, management and delivery of games lessons and how to develop games making; the yellow section deals with familiarization and skill challenges; the blue section with formal games and complementary practices; the green section with NGB mini-games. In addition 63 skill improvement cards are included to help teachers know what to look for as children are practising, and to enable children to help each other as they refine their skills. Sample lesson plans are also included. While intended for teachers, the resource should be of interest to anyone helping younger children to develop their ability in games. Figure 1 opposite identifies the game families and the games featured in the resource.

# FORMAL GAMES

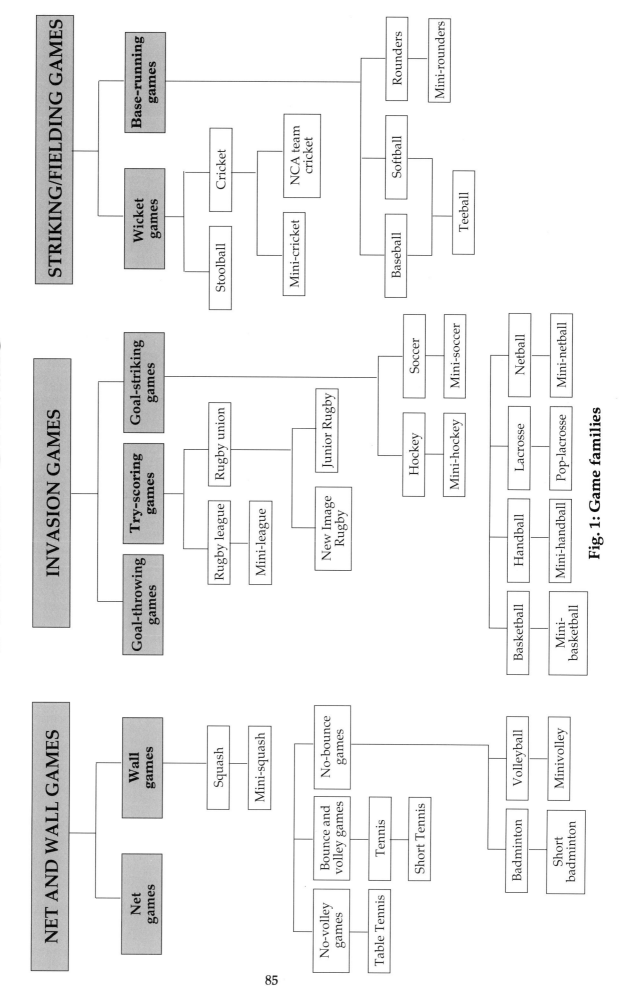

**Fig. 1: Game families**

As the consultancy developed, certain principles emerged to establish the philosophy underpinning the materials and guide the choice of content. These will be identified in turn and their relevance explained. However, I also used this opportunity to expand some of my own ideas.

## Principle 1

*Children should experience tasks which will enable them to demonstrate reasonable competence in the core skills by the age of seven.*

The core skills may be classified as:

| | |
|---|---|
| Locomotor | The player moves through space, eg. step, run, jump, slide, roll. |
| Non-locomotor | Specific parts of the body are moved while the player remains in one place. |
| Manipulative | Objects are moved using sending and collecting skills. |
| Combinations | Objects are moved as the player is travelling. |

The tasks should be challenging and incentive driven with children getting immediate feedback on their progress.

## Principle 2

*Children should become skilful within a range of games before specialising in selected games.*

Three elements contribute to being skilful in games. These are:

- Technical control of game objects.
- Physical capability.
- Insight, including an appreciation of game demands and how to meet those demands.

It is essential to pursue a progressive programme of work through the common core skills to game specific skills. This should recognise the pre-control, control, utilization, proficiency and exploitation stages of development. Figure 2 opposite provides a core skill spiral which illustrates these progressions. This spiral can be interpreted through a selected skill, eg. throwing and catching as shown in Figure 3 on page 88.

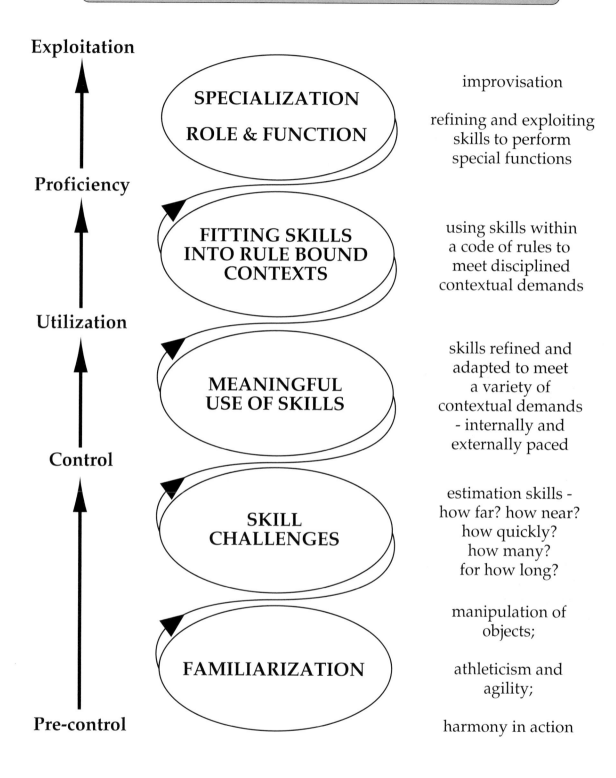

**Fig. 2: Core skill spiral – games**

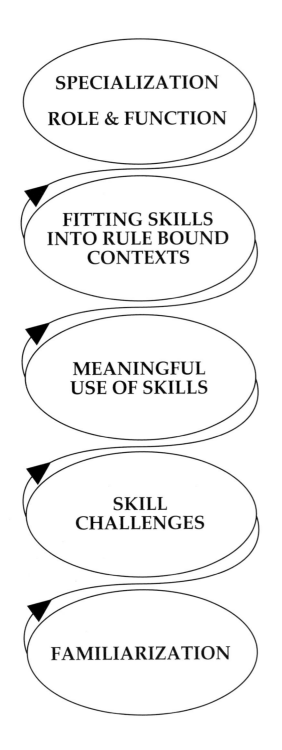

**SPECIALIZATION**

**ROLE & FUNCTION**

goalkeeping in soccer; cricket spin bowler; netball shooter; rugby scrum half etc.

**FITTING SKILLS INTO RULE BOUND CONTEXTS**

netball: throw within 3 secs.; rugby union: do not throw towards attacking line; basketball: obey travelling rule prior to passing or shooting.

**MEANINGFUL USE OF SKILLS**

passing involving coincidence skills and appropriate choice of technique; bowling; stumping; shooting; making safe; catching to dismiss a batter.

**SKILL CHALLENGES**

throwing to hit steady and erratic targets both near and far; throwing and catching quickly; catching an incoming ball on all sides of the body at different heights; catching off self, other and rebound feed

**FAMILIARIZATION**

holding, throwing and catching balls of different size, weight, shape and texture using either hand and both hands over a range of actions

**Fig. 3: Throw/catch spiral**

Maturation will take children to an elementary level of competence, but focused practice and appropriate teacher/coach interventions take children to a more mature level of proficiency. Creating suitable learning conditions, offering tasks which are relevant and appealing to the children, knowing what to look for and what to say or do to change performance, all unlock the door to improvement.

Children do not always appreciate the relevance or importance of athleticism in games. For example, during a lesson on sprinting a boy was avoiding his turn. When asked why this activity did not appeal to him he replied, 'I'm a footballer'. Similarly some children have no understanding of their role in a game as illustrated by one girl, who in a mini-hockey lesson, was standing at one end of the pitch well away from the focus of play. When asked what she was expected to do she replied, 'I dunno – teacher told me to stand here'. We do a disservice to learners if we do not embrace all three elements of skilfulness in our programmes of study – technical control, physical capability and insight.

## Principle 3

*NGB skill awards may complement the curriculum but testing should be undertaken outside lesson time.*

Materials and tasks associated with NGB skill awards can certainly help teachers/coaches to know what to look for and be updated with emerging skills, rules, etc. Children who wish to be tested should have the opportunity to do so outside lesson time, and ideally that testing should be supported by NGB personnel.

## Principle 4

*Children should understand the common intentions and demands of games within each game family.*

In addition to common skills all the games grouped within a game family have common characteristics. Figure 4 on the following page identifies common intentions and demands for each family of games. These statements hold true across all the games within a family so they can be used in the design of a core games programme in formal games. Formal games are those with rules determined by the teacher alone, by the teacher and the children together, or by the children alone. Children should be able to explain why their game falls into one or other of the game families and understand what they are expected to do within that game. As soon as they are ready to do so, children should be introduced to modified regulation games laid down by national governing bodies so that they may acquire specific game skills and appreciate the significance of set rules.

# THE COMMON INTENTIONS AND DEMANDS OF THE GAME FAMILIES NET/WALL, INVASION AND STRIKING/FIELDING

## NET GAMES
**Intention:**

To score by hitting a ball or shuttlecock into the opposing court so that it cannot be returned to land in your court.

**Demands:**

To hit the ball into the opposing court in order to move opponents and make space to make a winning shot.

To hit the ball using placement, pace, flight, spin and disguise so that it is difficult for opponents to return, so forcing them to make an error.

To deny opponents space in your court area through maintaining a good 'ready' position from which to move to all parts of the court and be comfortably placed to hit the ball or shuttlecock.

## WALL GAMES
**Intention:**

To strike a ball against a wall or walls so that it cannot be returned by an opponent.

To reach a pre-determined score before an opponent.

**Demands:**

To decide where to play the ball in order to score or disadvantage an opponent.

To play the ball accurately to the chosen target with suitable pace on the ball.

To position to dominate the court area and give easier access to the ball.

To have the agility, athleticism and endurance to meet game demands.

## INVASION GAMES
**Intentions:**

To score by manoeuvring a ball through defended territory to an agreed target.

To prevent the opposing team from scoring in the target you are defending.

To have the higher score at the end of play. Game time having been decided beforehand.

**Demands:**

To respond to the ebb and flow of play as determined by possession in a shared playing area.

When in possession of the ball to progress it towards the target and create and convert scoring opportunities.

To keep and move the ball both individually and in co-operation with team-mates.

When the opponents have the ball to prevent them from creating and converting scoring opportunities, whilst trying to regain possession.

To counter the actions of opponent(s) both individually and in co-operation with team-mates.

To recognize game problems, consider possible solutions, recall previous responses and make best-bet choices.

To have the speed, agility and technical control to respond effectively within the time/space pressures imposed by a game.

To have the fitness to sustain effort throughout the game.

## STRIKING/FIELDING GAMES
**Overall Intention:**

To have the highest possible score over a prescribed number of innings.

**Intentions of Batting Team:**

To hit a ball delivered by an opponent.

To score by running to or round fixed markers or by sending the ball out of the bounded playing area.

**Intentions of Fielding Team:**

To prevent batsmen from scoring.

To get batsmen out.

**Demands Placed on Batting Team:**

To prevent the delivered ball from beating the bat.

To strike the ball away from fielders and set up scoring opportunities.

To run between or round the markers before the fielders can return the ball.

**Demands Placed on Fielding Team:**

To deliver the ball to the striker so that it is difficult to hit and/or force an error which leads to no score or a dismissal.

To get to the struck ball quickly to restrict the score and/or dismiss a striker.

Brenda Read
Loughborough University
June 1992

**Fig. 4: The common intentions and demands of the game families**

**Principle 5**

*The games curriculum should be game centred and practice tasks should reflect game demands.*

Games give skills their meaning. It used to be common practice to adopt a technique centred approach to games teaching with lessons following the regular pattern of warm-up, skill practice, game. While this is acceptable practice it rarely enables children to connect what they have been practising with what they are required to do in the game. Figure 5 below illustrates this technique centred approach.

# A TRADITIONAL TECHNIQUE-LED APPROACH TO THE TEACHING OF GAMES

**Lesson format**
Warm-up
Technique development
Game

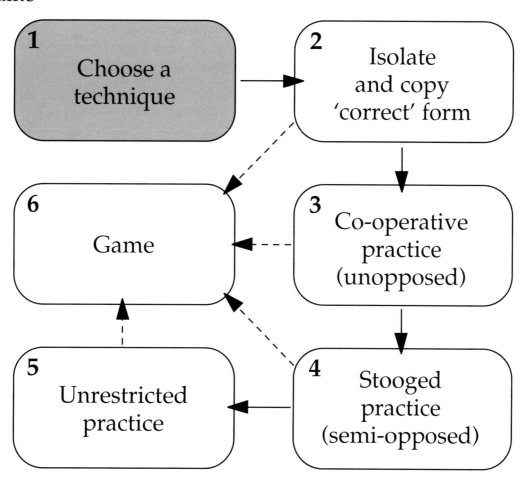

**Fig. 5: A traditional technique-led approach to the teaching of games**

91

Because of adjustments we can now make to game rules, playing equipment, playing areas and so on, it is no longer necessary for the teaching of techniques always to precede game play. The following examples show the adjustments we can make in net games to make the game accessible to all pupils:

- Kinder equipment, eg. slow bounce balls, short handled, lightweight, large faced rackets.
- Rule changes, eg. serve from midway down the court in short tennis, the ball may bounce once or twice.
- Playing area, eg. you play in a smaller court than your opponent, raise the net to slow the game.

Good technique is important but we should try to adopt an approach which brings a game alive and involves children in problem-solving and testing ideas, as well as in the mastery of required skills. Figure 6 below presents a game centred approach to teaching games.

## A GAME CENTRED APPROACH TO TEACHING GAMES

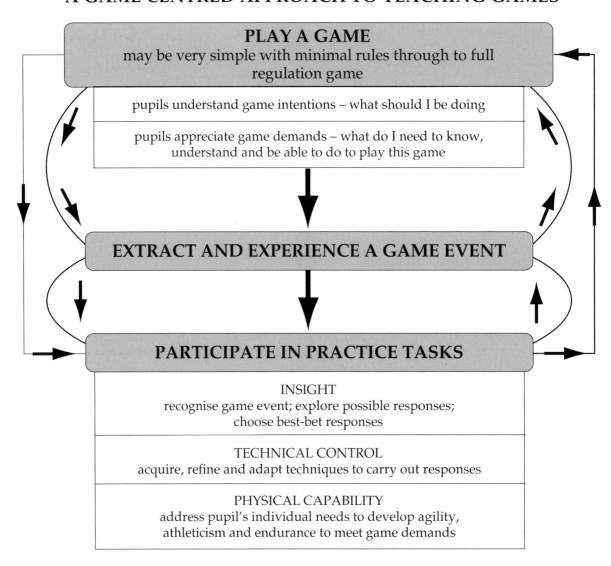

Fig. 6: A game centred approach to teaching games

The logical sequence of activity is:

- play a game – this may be very simple or a full regulation game played to strict rules
- extract an event from the game, that is, a situation which reappears from time to time, eg. a player with a chance to go solo and take the ball past a defender in mini-hockey, or one player at the net and the other on the baseline in short tennis
- participate in practice tasks to acquire and refine the technical control or physical capability or insight to meet game demands
- return to the extracted game event or the game to test progress.

By establishing this connection between game demands and what is practised the children learn to recognise where skills 'fit' in the game, what their role is in the game and how that role relates to other players.

### Principle 6

*Adult regulation games are not appropriate for children in games lessons before the age of 11.*

Simplified or reduced games give children lots of opportunity to be involved close to the focus of play, where they can test and exploit their developing skills many times. Although children aged 9-11 may mimic adults in full regulation games, they rarely have charge of their involvement in that game. Talented and/or interested children should be given access to full regulation games outside lesson time as appropriate.

### Principle 7

*Children should become independent learners, assume ownership of their decisions and accept responsibility for their actions.*

I recollect an interview with a coach who, when asked why his talented soccer team was unexpectedly losing 1-0 replied, 'they forget what they have been told'. Teachers and coaches need to be prepared to shift the ownership decisions to the children by acquainting them with the 'what if' aspect of playing games, and by involving them in tasks which offer an opportunity to explore game ideas; helping pupils to see things in different ways and accommodate the unexpected. It should be the intention of every teacher and coach to make themselves redundant as the learners gradually assume control of their performance.

We need to free players to use their imagination and 'play' games. The child who comes to class wearing a Liverpool shirt is John Barnes for that lesson; two children playing short tennis may be enacting a fantasy Wimbledon final; a cricket bowler may be visualising and imitating the action of a favourite player. To imagine is to dream, to look beyond what is to what might be. To be free to make mistakes and profit from them. To have the skill, impudence, agility, athleticism and conviction to enjoy and benefit from playing games. Hopefully 'Teaching Children to Play Games 5-11: A Resource for Primary Teachers' [1] will lead the way.

1   Available from Coachwise Ltd, Leeds – Tel: 0532 743889.

# Creating a Network

## David M Shaw

*David Shaw was appointed National Youth Development Officer for the Rugby Football Union in 1989. He has been a Club and County player and was an RFU Staff Coach until 1985, when he was appointed Divisional Technical Administrator. He has made numerous contributions to RFU technical publications and videos.*

### Summary of Presentation

Access rates for youngsters have altered, owing to the changing role of education, competition from other sports, and demographic changes. The emphasis is now on the voluntary clubs to help in facilitating both the entry of young people to the sport, and their development within it.

Points addressed in the presentation included:

- the role of partnerships
- aspects of the Youth Development Officer's job
- access routes, both for coaches and youngsters
- club-school links
- promotional support
- educational support materials.

It is to be hoped that the new strategy will result in expanding numbers, age group levels, school affiliations and women's teams; these changes will be underpinned by coach development.

Illustrations of activities from clubs working with YDOs were shown as models of good practice. In the future it is hoped that expansion will lead to the development of performance/excellence, and the introduction of regional co-ordinators. However, these plans should be rationalised by the need to assemble adequate funding packages.

Voluntary clubs should link with schools and local authorities in order to provide appropriate recreational opportunities for young people. Governing Bodies also need to assist in providing the structure, resources and promotional support materials to underpin their activities and provide for the next generation of players.

*The easiest part of development work is motivating the youngsters.*
*Without adequate structures and coaching support we only open windows.*
*Through them we can offer pathways of participation and then excellence.*

# Nurturing Talent – East German Style

## Peter Sutcliffe

*In his work with the Sports Council, Peter Sutcliffe was heavily involved in Sports Development, establishing Centres of Excellence in fourteen different sports. Coach education and supplementary fund raising were also part of his brief. In his role as Head of Facilities Unit, Peter assisted in drawing up Manchester's first Olympic bid. He has published numerous articles on Cricket and Sport in Eastern Europe and is currently working on a book on GDR Sport.*

The Television Tower in East Berlin, like sport in East Germany, was meant to symbolise a modern, socialist state, capable of matching Western capitalist countries and West Germany, in particular. When the Wall came down a very different picture was revealed.

The German Democratic Republic was bankrupt, not only economically, but perhaps more crucially, spiritually and morally. Every aspect of life in East Germany was dominated by 'The Party' and its all-pervading, but grossly inefficient bureaucracy. Society was riddled with deception, dishonesty and hypocrisy. Some 15% of the population was estimated to have been police informers. Industrial pollution was approaching epidemic proportions.

In contrast, despite, or maybe a contributory factor to the *status quo*, East German sport was enjoying ever increasing success in the world's sporting arenas.

When I photographed the tower, six years ago, little did I suspect its irony. The reflection is cast in a window of the Palast Hotel, a hotel for western tourists which, like sport in the GDR, was a smoke screen created to obscure the reality of life in East Germany. Access to the hotel was off limits to almost all East Germans.

Access to the best sports facilities in the GDR was also off limits to all but a small number of highly privileged performers. Sport, no less than staying at the best hotels, was not an egalitarian activity. No more than .2% of the population or approximately 35,000 top class sportsmen, women and children, were involved in the GDR's elite sports system. Yet recent estimates indicate that almost 10% of the GDR's GNP was spent on sport – most of it on this privileged .2%.

At international level, the policy paid off. In Olympic and World competition, the GDR was 33 times and 34 times as successful as the USA and USSR respectively, ie. in terms of medals won per head of population. More significantly, for East Germany's political leaders as we shall see, it was 16 times more successful than West Germany. Putting this into a British context, in only four Olympics in which the GDR competed as a single nation, its tally of medals outstripped that of Britain, despite us being one of the few nations to have competed in every Olympics since 1896.

It is useless to ask **how** such results were obtained, unless we also ask **why** sporting success was so vital for East Germany. Only then can we understand what led a relatively small nation to take on the world's sporting giants and look for some justification for its profligate and draconian policy of sportpolitik.

In order to do this we must briefly step back into history. In 1945 Germany was a defeated, guilt ridden and devastated nation. The Potsdam Treaty partitioned Germany into four Occupied Zones, and ceded a sizeable proportion of its former territory to the Soviet Union and Poland. In the Soviet Zone, swingeing war reparations further debilitated German life.

By contrast, the Americans set about rebuilding the Western Zones, both economically and socially, but according to a very determined Western democratic philosophy.

Nor must we forget Germany's distinguished sporting tradition stretching back two centuries, to Guths Muths in the 18th Century and Friedrich Jahn in the 19th Century. It was natural, therefore, for the Western Allies to encourage sport and physical education as part of a rehabilitation exercise, perhaps in order to overcome more recent and sinister Nazi associations with sport.

A National Olympic Committee was formed, albeit with a membership which strongly resembled its pre-war Nazi counterpart. The President was Ritter von Halt, Hitler's former Reichsportfuhrer. The Secretary was Carl Diem, the organiser of the 1936 Olympics. And who can excuse or forget the first political hijacking of a world sporting event, Hitler's Berlin Olympics?

In direct contrast, the Soviet Union banned all former sports organisations in its zone, except those sponsored by Socialist or Communist associations. Since their organisation and personnel were less than sympathetic to former Fascists the seeds of dispute between sport in the East and West had already been sown.

The Soviet authorities treated competitive sport with suspicion, believing that it encouraged nationalism. Thus the first associations in the Soviet Zone were strictly controlled. Competition was banned on the grounds that it encouraged nationalism. One of the early organisers was Manfred Ewald, later to become the authoritarian functionary of East German sport. He cleverly disguised his former Fascist connections, having been the leader of the Hitler Youth in Mecklenburg. He now embraced 'Socialism' as opposed to 'National Socialism'. I have been told that, like St Paul, his conversion was genuine, but like many converts his subsequent behaviour was over-zealous, to say the least.

By May 1949 Allied relations had deteriorated to such an extent that the West decided to go it alone and form a new German state in their three zones – the Federal Republic – in direct contravention of the Potsdam Treaty. After six months of recriminations the Soviet Union went ahead with the formation of the German Democratic Republic. In the ensuing forty years the two Germanies were in direct opposition being both the centre and victims of a 'Cold War', bitterly contested by the former Allies.

A number of East/West political crises triggered off disputes between the parallel German sports bodies. First, in June 1948, the Soviet Union cut West Berlin's supply routes by land, from the remainder of West Germany. For a year, supplies were shipped in by air – the Berlin airlift – this at a time when the sports bodies were seeking areas of cooperation. Negotiations were aborted.

In 1951 the GDR formed its own National Olympic Committee (NOC). Also in that year West Germany was accepted into membership of the United Nations. East Germany was refused membership. The so-called German NOC, in reality, the West German NOC was accepted into membership of the IOC, along with the Soviet Union. Three weeks later the GDR was refused membership, on the grounds, said the IOC, that the Soviet Zone was not a separate state but merely an area of land, and in any case, there was already one German Olympic Committee.

It was this series of humiliating rejections which proved decisive for the subsequent direction of GDR sport; it was to become a political tool rather than a social concept.

Walter Ulbricht, then East Germany's most powerful leader and lifelong sports enthusiast, sponsored a decree in the Volkskammer, to the effect that East German sport was to be developed in order to dominate West German sport. Although subject to considerable scepticism, he stated that 'East German sportsmen and women would become diplomats in track suits, standing on the winning rostra of the world'. Less overtly, it was also decided that sport would be used to buy influence throughout the third world, particularly in North and Central Africa.

Although Ulbricht did not live to see his vision realised he was vindicated. The German Democratic Republic became a member of the United Nations in 1972, largely on the strength of an Arab/African vote. In that same year, again with crucial support from Arab countries in the IOC, East Germany first marched into an Olympic stadium (Munich) under its own banner and to its own anthem.

East Germany was now one of the world's great sporting nations. Its system was described as a miracle machine. But was it? Germany had achieved as much once before in the 1936 Olympics, winning 40 medals, 16 more than its nearest rival the USA, and 35 more than it had achieved four years earlier in Los Angeles.

What was the secret? In 1951, it was the same as in Nazi Germany, unstinting political support which provided resources and backing – but at the cost of total subservience to a political doctrine; in 1932, Fascism, in 1951 Stalinism.

Planning was meticulous. The first step was to establish a teaching institute, which would train university teachers and administrators to build up the sports system. The second stage of the institute's work was to train a cadre of professional coaches, with a depth of academic knowledge about sport and a capacity to direct and understand research into top level performance. The third task was to set up a research institute to guide coaches and governing bodies of sport on methods and policy. The final task was to train medical personnel, doctors and physiotherapists to support coaches and athletes. In 1951 the German University of Physical Culture (or DHfK), at Leipzig was founded by Ulbricht, to fulfil all of these objectives. For obvious reasons it became known as the 'Red College'.

From humble beginnings, 14 staff and 96 students housed in primitive accommodation with few books or materials, it grew into a world famous institute with upwards of 2000 students and 600 staff, at any one time, including 80 with professorships. A research institute employed 350 sports scientists and directed research projects with each national governing body of sport.

Courses were extended from eight months to two years, three years and finally, in 1956, to four years. Initially staff studied in the Soviet Union and Soviet teachers worked at the DHfK.

A modular correspondence system was established in conjunction with six other institutes of higher education to cater for the coaching aspirations of current athletes within the elite sports club system. At any one time, upwards of 1000 such students would be engaged in courses of study lasting between six and twelve years.

Throughout this time they were paid 80% of the salary of a fully-qualified coach, ensuring that the best sportsmen and women remained in the system, ploughing back invaluable expertise and experience.

Entry to the coach education system was limited to the predicted number of coaches required, so that future employment was guaranteed. All prospective students required the 'Abitur', the equivalent of our 'A' level.

Ulbricht's policy of 'sportpolitik' increasingly slanted coach education and research towards elite sport. Students were required to be members of the Free German Youth, and staff could not progress unless they joined the Party. Students and staff were required to attend political briefings three times per month, in their own time. Within the College course, 300 hours over eight semesters were devoted to a study of Marxism/Leninism.

Individuals, staff and students were secretly recruited by the Stasi as informers. The publication of research findings, or even their discussion amongst colleagues, was strictly forbidden. No coach could work in the elite sports system unless employed by the State or without an academic qualification from the DHfK.

It is interesting that one of the GDR's first areas of development should have been coach education and research rather than the obvious, but simplistic, concern for the athletes.

Running parallel to coach education was the establishment of a sport bureaucracy closely allied to the political system. In fact, one which mirrored the party political structure and allowed for, or rather demanded, cross representation at all levels.

The East Germans took a pragmatic approach, first trying to organise sport through the youth movement, whose secretary at that time was Eric Honecker, guided by the German Sports Committee, in a similar way to the Soviet experiment with the Komsomol. It failed to be replaced in 1956 by the DTSB, the German Gymnastic and Sports Association. All previous structures were swept away overnight, without redress. Imagine the furore in Britain, if the government attempted to replace all of our National Governing Bodies and Local Authority sports provision. Note the structure of the DTSB. Under the leadership of Manfred Ewald it controlled all sports activity, but concentrated especially on elite sport. It controlled the coaches, the clubs, the national governing bodies of sport, the NOC, the sports schools and sports medicine, because it held the purse strings. In turn it was subservient to the Central Committee, on which Ewald served together with the Minister for Sport, latterly Gunther Erbach. It is interesting to note that sport, as of right, held two key cabinet positions. In addition, the Minister for Internal Security, Erich Mielke, the second most powerful figure in the Central Committee, was a sports fanatic, so much so that he lived in a suite of rooms at the Dynamo SC in Berlin.

When the East German sports strategy was in the planning stage, a group of men, all of whom later became key figures in the sports establishment, spent six weeks studying the Soviet sports system. One area of especial interest was the growing number of sports schools in the Soviet Union. The East Germans took the best of the Russian system and added some ideas of their own.

Over the years several simple principles have been applied with ruthless efficiency:

- Every sports school should be associated with an adult sports club, with a common, professional, coaching staff, to ensure a continuity from school to adult sport.
- Complete coverage of the country was required. Those children with travel problems would board.
- Education and sports coaching had to be carefully coordinated.
- Only two criteria for entry should be applied, political reliability and sporting potential. Failure to live up to expectations in either would result in expulsion.
- The system would be limited to the numbers needed to fulfil the demands of national teams in the so-called, medal intensive sports.
- All necessary facilities and back-up, eg. sports medicine, pools, ice, to be provided.
- Schools/clubs would specialise, even within the range of medal intensive sports, in order to economise on coaching staff and facilities.

At the time of the political changes a network of twenty-five schools/clubs had been established.

Before giving examples of the organisation of schools and clubs and their scale of resources in terms of staff and facilities, I should like to indicate the pathways by which children were selected and sustained in the elite sports system. As always in the GDR, we must first look at the plan.

Each four year Olympic cycle, targets of achievement were set for each sport based on a points system, with maximum points for Olympic success, and in descending order, winning World, European, National, Regional down to County titles, with scaled points for the first six places.

The pyramid of achievement gives a guide. Different organisations in the sports system qualified for points, the NGB of the sport concerned, the KJS or club training the athlete and so on. Future funding depended on achieving the targets. Bonuses were available for exceeding the targets. Underachievement was punished. Thus pressure was endemic to the system, more so since the targets were set by a joint committee representing the SED's Central Committee and the DTSB.

Similarly the numbers of children entering the system was based on long term planning. No more came in than would be required to meet the targets. Occasionally things went wrong; injury and loss of form to girl gymnasts in the mid eighties led to insufficient numbers of competitors in the system.

The Pyramid had other implications. There was a statutory requirement for employers to release post school athletes for training in their clubs, sixteen hours per week in the Masterclass, eight in Class One and four in Class Two. Employers were financially compensated by the DTSB for loss of working time.

Potential entry into the elite sports system began in the kindergarten, with children aged 3-6 years old. Most kindergarten teachers were three years trained, with PE qualifications. Physically gifted children at this age were drawn to the attention of coaches at the nearest KJS/SC. Those sufficiently motivated were then invited to attend a Training Centre, the age geared to the physical demands of the sport. Every district had a centre for each medal intensive sport.

From the kindergarten, children moved to an all age polytechnical school at the age of seven. From this age, all physical education lessons were taught by four-year trained specialist teachers. Talented children missed at an earlier age, or those showing promise at sports introduced at a later stage in their physical development, were sifted out by specialist coaches and invited to the training centre. In the unlikely circumstance of anyone of promise being missed, a further avenue came via the industrial sports club, or from inter-district competition which led up to the bi-annual Spartakiade, more of which shortly.

Children in the Training Centres were constantly assessed and those with the best diagnostic predictions for future success were invited for further screening before being offered a place at a KJS. Screening varied from sport to sport, involving skill assessments, physiological tests for adaptation to exercise and a general medical examination. Intellectual achievement formed part of the assessment along with a strict survey of the family's political reliability. Any child with a close relative in the West was ineligible.

Age of entry to a KJS differed from sport to sport: diving, skating and gymnastics around seven, swimming eleven, weight-lifting and sailing around thirteen and fourteen. Those children leaving school at the age of sixteen to go into industry or vocational training however, could live in a residential block in the club if they so wished. Since alternative accommodation was limited this was often the case. Those going on to take Abitur remained at school to the age of nineteen or twenty, being given one or two extra years to achieve the required academic level. The only parental requirement was total commitment, political orthodoxy, ie. support for the party, and twenty marks per month for those in residential accommodation.

In the West, criticism of this system has been severe, and to some extent can be justified. However, too often it has been based on hearsay or on the comments of those who have defected and, therefore, are not likely to offer an objective judgement. Almost uniquely, for a Westerner, I have visited three such schools and looked at one of them in great detail. My observations would not support such judgements, other than on the question of drug abuse, more of which later. I also base my judgement on residential teaching experience in our own Public School system.

The Rostock KJS played an important part in the life of the city, where it was held in great esteem, not to say affection. Few inhabitants were untouched by its activities, as children, parents, teachers or supporters.

Academic classes were grouped according to sport and age. School work in the mornings was followed by training in the afternoons, with more training and private study in the evenings – a long day. The Rostock school shared excellent facilities with the Club; a sports hall, an indoor athletic track, a 50m pool with diving well, a synthetic track and a shale track, a 60m x 30m ice rink, gymnastic training areas and specialist rooms for individual sports. The general public had only very limited access to these facilities. In addition there was a medical centre catering solely for school and club members.

To remain at a KJS, children had to meet stringent norms not only in their sport, but also in academic achievement. Any youngster falling behind was given six months grace to regain lost ground, after which time it was back to the polytechnical school. Because the sports schools attracted the best teachers, children were seldom academically disadvantaged by the system, but inevitably, there was a sense of failure in having to leave.

The boarding houses were comfortable and very well supervised within a House Parental system. Each child had a 'house mother', always a qualified teacher, often in physical education, but whose duties were purely pastoral.

At the time of the political changes, it had been recognised that the system was wasteful. Children should have been given more grace to catch up, or alternatively, more opportunity to change sports. There are examples of where this was successful. Karen Anke changed from middle distance running to speed skating, and was rewarded with Olympic Gold. In contrast, the swimmer Roger Pittel told me that of 30 eleven year olds recruited to his group in Leipzig, he was the only survivor at the age of 16. Various estimates of success rates have been given; probably no more than 20% survived to be senior competitors. However, many so-called failures gravitated to sports medicine, physiotherapy and allied disciplines. Some even became coaches.

Another criticism is over specialisation, again with some justification. Children had little opportunity to play anything other than their main sport. And of course, pressure to perform, imposed by the system was felt by children, teachers and coaches alike.

Training centred around the bi-annual Spartakiade, held alternatively in Berlin and Leipzig. The Leipzig festival was combined with inter-county competitions for adults in the factory sports clubs. Ten thousand children and fifty thousand adults took part in the 1987 Leipzig event, the last to be held in the GDR. I was fortunate to be there.

Typically it was both a sporting and a political event. The whole of the Central Committee attended the opening events, day and night on the first day. The opening event was very similar to that of the 1936 Olympics. In addition there were a number of international events to bring added prestige to the festival.

The following points should be made at this juncture:

- All the youngsters were given the chance to feel the atmosphere of major competition from an early age.
- The competitions gave coaches and children alike the experience of peaking for a major event.
- Potential champions were identified at an early age.
- A major event of this kind gave a shop window to advertise GDR sport to the world. Five hundred overseas guests attended, each representing his own association, including members of the IOC. Sir Arthur Gold represented the IAAF at the opening ceremony.
- The enormous prestige of a major festival not only reflected well on sport in the GDR, but sought to legitimise its elaborate structure and cost in the eyes of the public.
- By identifying with the Spartakiade, the Party was seen to support and be an integral part of a highly successful venture, all part of creating the illusion of a benevolent, paternalistic political leadership.

The penultimate building block in the elite sports system was the sports club. Much has already been said about them and their association with the KJS network.

All internal competition in the GDR was based around the 25 elite sports clubs. It was impossible for an athlete to be selected from outside this structure. Clubs were sponsored by both state and industry. Their facilities lacked nothing which would contribute to success. They also provided the raw material for research, technical, physiological and psychological. By and large the general public had, at best, limited access to their facilities, and in some cases, none at all.

A case in point was the Dynamo SC in Berlin. It was sponsored by the internal security forces of the city, the Stasi. Mielke, the Minister for State Security poured millions of Ost-marks into the club. Sharing the same site were two KJSs, the Werner Seelenbinder KJS and the Ernst Grube KJS, and the TSC SC. In addition the security forces did their own physical training on site.

Finally, we come to the most discredited aspect of East German sport – the sports medical service, allied to the Research Institute at Leipzig and its outpost at Kreisha, which ironically was also the drug testing centre for the GDR, acting on behalf of the international sports bodies, not least of which was the IOC.

Would-be sports doctors trained in internal medicine for three years, along with trainees for other medical specialisms in standard medical schools. Three further years were spent studying sports medicine, under the guidance of specialists in Leipzig. There, doctors trained alongside coaches, gaining valuable experience of competitive sport. On graduation they were allocated responsibilities within the system, in clubs, governing bodies of sport or, perhaps, district clinics. Not all worked in the elite sports system.

A minority of doctors specialised in particular sports, soccer, swimming, throwing events etc. Over 60 worked at the Dynamo SC, where necessary carrying out major surgery on sportsmen and women, in addition to routine, minor treatments.

But what do we know about the less savoury part of their work, the use of drugs – notably, but not exclusively, anabolic steroids. Quite a lot, following recent revelations.

In her recent book – *Doping*, Brigitte Berendonk, formerly an East German Olympic athlete and sports doctor who defected to the West, documents the whole shameful saga, even noting collusion between the DTSB and the Central Committee represented by Eric Honecker, no less. Her book confirms other recent revelations in the West German media.

First to break cover, in *Stern*, was Aschenbach, a former GDR ski-jumper and sports doctor. He was followed by Hoppner, one of East Germany's acknowledged experts in the use of steroids. Finally, Riedel, said to be the arch doper of GDR track and field athletes, came into the open. Incidentally, Riedel now, and I quote, 'follows a remarkably successful career in West Germany', in a university teaching hospital. His medical research centred on the use of drugs to enhance performance in jumping events. He is alleged to have been closely associated with Heike Drechsler.

All sources admit that doping, since the 70s, has been part of a national conspiracy orchestrated by the DTSB and encouraged by the Party.

Justification was sought in the excuse that drugs were a world-wide sporting phenomena. It is also claimed that no lasting side effects of drugs have been seen in GDR athletes, because medical supervision was part of the overall control of an athlete's training and preparation for competition. Of course, it may yet be too early to assess the long term effects of drugs, but Berendonk notes that short term side effects were common. A testimony to the close medical monitoring of athletes is indicated by the fact that only two GDR athletes have ever tested positive in competition and none since 1979. Since 1980, 38 Americans have failed official drug tests after competition.

The East Germans signally failed to accept that:

- the use of drugs is forbidden by all the world's sporting bodies
- to administer steroids to young people under the age of 18 was against GDR law.

Michael Regner, a former East German national coach for swimming puts the system into perspective. He said, 'The taking of steroids was controlled by a central commission in Berlin, as part of a systematic programme to enhance physical development. The timing and dosage of steroids was specified for **every** athlete in the system, to be administered by the coaches, who had to submit annual reports on the results.'

He continued, 'the specialised training of talented youngsters coupled with the use of steroids, catapulted them, at the age of 14 or 15, into world class swimmers. Without drugs they would never have achieved such results.'

And so the evidence builds up: Hannemann, a former European silver medallist further identified the use of hormones, androgens, with young girls. Details are contained in a secret report published in 1988 called 'State Plan, topic 14.25.' It states that 10mg of Oral-Turinabol should be standard for 14-15 year old girls. Dosages were based on the research findings of Drs Rademacher and Baumgart at the Research Institute in Leipzig, where it is alleged that up to 20% of research output was devoted to the use of drugs.

Berendonk makes the point that the GDR's women athletes, throwers in particular, consumed unbelievable dosages of steroids. She even lists them in order of consumption. Top of the list is Inies Muller/Reichenbach, from Rostock, a World Bronze medallist in the shot in 1987, with a career best of 3,680 mg of Oral-Turinabol. Even the list of GDR pharmaceutical suppliers is listed. Need I continue with this sorry tale?

I began this paper by saying that East German society was riddled with deception, dishonesty and hypocrisy. How, therefore, could we expect sport to be immune from the wider moral decay? After all, we would claim sport to be part of the fabric of society.

For example, athletes, like other members of society, were recruited as informers by the Stasi, to spy on fellow athletes and especially to report on contacts with westerners during those privileged trips beyond 'The Wall'.

And what of 'The Wall'; it was built in 1961 in order to preserve the integrity of the East German state. At that time 50,000 people, mostly under 25, were crossing to West Berlin every month. Resources in terms of cash and goods were flowing out of the GDR at an alarming rate, due to an imbalance in currency values and speculation.

Many of these problems had been created by the policies of the Western Allies and West Germany, quite deliberately as part of the 'Cold War'. The West has some responsibility for the Wall. Similarly, to an extent, the denial of national sovereignty by the West in the United Nations and the IOC drove East Germany to the excesses we now recognise.

But to return to sport, few athletes resisted the use of steroids. Drugs were seen to be necessary for success and that's what athletes were in sport for. Many welcomed them. Marita Koch is on record as complaining that her sister athletes were getting more and better steroids than she was.

Although payments at that time were against the amateur statutes of most Olympic sports, GDR athletes were pleased to accept up to 25,000 marks, twice the annual salary of a worker, for winning Olympic Gold. Prize money was on an officially listed sliding scale. They could also qualify for better housing, or that final accolade, a Trabbie. Athletes and coaches were further seduced by luxury cruises to the Caribbean, while their fellow citizens were confined to Eastern Europe. Sport was the thing to be in, as an athlete, coach or educator. So how shall we judge its participants?

Over the last six years I have known and become close friends with a number of East Germans from the system. The daughter of one of those six men who first went to the Soviet Union in 1951 is spending a year with my family at the present time. I know Marita Koch and many others. By and large, they seem decent, honest members of society. But in the words of one of them 'I was no hero'. Bit by bit he was flattered by his growing status in sport, which itself was gaining international prestige and status. But there is seldom anything without a price. Standards and morals were slowly eroded as the Party called in its dues.

What would have been unimaginable in 1950 had become commonplace thirty years later.

At the outset many had been committed socialists, but by the time disillusionment had crept in, they were enmeshed in a political system which used coercion as its main ingredient. Resistance brought professional disgrace, not only on a personal level, but for the family. Acceptance brought security and a privileged place in society. Resistance brought the tread on the stairs and that dreaded knock on the door from a member of the Stasi – I wonder where we would have stood.

In conclusion, I would ask you to take away an impression of what was good in the system, not only the corruption.

Talent could blossom, regardless of parental support and financial backing – ask our tennis authorities about the implications here. Athletes could train and compete without losing out educationally or professionally. Coaching was accepted as a skilled and well rewarded profession. Sports science was an integral part of performance, as if 20% of research went on drug use, 80% went on legitimate scientific back up. These are just a few of the benefits.

With the crumbling of the wall, so the Party crumbled along with the elements which had sustained it, including sport, but is this the end of the story in the new Germany? Maybe not. Watch this space.

However, for those involved in sport, perhaps the moral of this little tale is 'beware politicians bearing gifts'.

# Young People: Keeping them Involved

## Malcolm Tungatt

*Malcolm Tungatt is the leader of the Sports Council's In-House Research Team, monitoring and evaluating a programme of projects pioneering sports development in the community and establishing new partnerships. He has led the team since early 1987 and has co-ordinated the dissemination of the results.*

### Introduction

My title today says it all. Keeping young people involved in sport is probably the most productive way of increasing overall participation. It is this process that builds on the hard work of parents, teachers and sports enthusiasts in introducing young people to sport. Without it, this enthusiasm can often be wasted.

I shall concentrate on the 14-18 age range, but it's important that we begin with a reminder of their sporting backgrounds. I'm going to review some of the 'myths and realities' about young people to set the scene, and then I've been asked to look at the role of the teacher, the role of the school environment, the role of the sports community in general, and of particular relevance to most of you, the role of the coach in keeping youngsters involved.

Six themes will form the basis of my presentation:

- The myths and realities.
- How do children get involved in casual sport?
- Why are we all particularly concerned with the 'performance kids'?
- Why is 'coach education' so important when working with young people, and why is the coach a vital part of the sports development continuum?
- Why do we need to co-ordinate our efforts, particularly through the governing bodies?
- Why the recent emphasis on Youth Sport Managers; what I have previously called the 'focus of opportunity'.

I'll finish with a personal view of the way ahead; the way to keep our 14-18 year olds committed to their sporting interests.

### Young People – What do they Want from Sport?

Let's begin with the young people. I'm convinced that keeping them involved is all about understanding them. Their sporting interests; their aspirations; their attitudes towards sport and, for all of you, their attitudes towards performance and getting better.

We must understand the current generation; ravers and ecstasy; music and videos that are unintelligible unless you are on a dance floor; computer games and graphics; everything is 'wicked', and that has only recently replaced 'well-bad' and 'cool'.

And sport? 24-hour SKY-sport and SKY-sport plus; Channel 4's minority sports; American Football: 'Let's play ball, OK, let's play ball. Let's get some enthusiasm out there'; even the BBC, which won the 'Golden Rings' award for the best television coverage of the 1992 Olympics – beating CBS, NBC and the Japanese.

Sport in high profile. Our kids get a deluge of sport in all its forms – M & S clothing, computer sports games and the 'real thing'; GCSE PE, 'A level' PE, and 'education for leisure' in personal and social development lessons.

So what are the myths that live on?

Let's go back to the typical scenario, which goes something like this:

- Many young people do not get a worthwhile and meaningful introduction to physical activity at Primary School.
- As they get older, young people are supposed to be switched off sport by their PE lessons in Secondary School, particularly the girls and young women.
- As a result it is commonly believed that most young people give up sport on leaving school because they don't see it as relevant.
- In order to overcome this 'switch off' from the sports they have experienced at school, young people are thought to need to know more about the range of sports that are around when they leave school if they are to take part.
- Secondly, those that are keen to play will need to know where they can play casually and how to join clubs.
- For the committed players, they will need to know where to go to get better at their sports.
- They will need to know more about how to book places to play, how to set up clubs and their own groups and how to meet other players.

Finally, if they do drop out, they need a programme of positive action to attract them back.

Now I shall go back and look at the reality of these conclusions and reactions to the issues.

Firstly, what is the primary experience really like? Well, it is often true that many primary age children do not get the ideal foundation. Put quite simply, the primary teachers are struggling to deliver PE in the national curriculum, but it is not their fault. The subject is a threat to them; outdoors, apparatus, control problems and safety factors. We really do need to support our primary colleagues, not just with resources, but with involvement. We have to make them part of our network if secondary teachers and coaches are to inherit the Year 7s we would all like to see each September. If they're turned-off at seven, what chance at 14? But, in the main, the research shows they are enthusiastic. This reaction from our survey of nine year olds in Dudley is typical:

*PE is good. I like the stretching and jogging too.*
*And we like to show good things and it's fun and exciting.*

Are we going to switch them off again in our Secondary Schools? Well no, at least not the majority. From our survey of nearly 1,000 young people in Coventry, the evidence is that most of them had been switched on by their PE lessons.

Eighty nine percent had identified a sport that they had enjoyed in their PE lessons. Although they had experienced 15-20 sports during the five years at Secondary School, it wasn't the choice or range of sports on offer that was important, it was the context, style and presentation that mattered to them and the reasons for enjoying the sports reflect this.

|  | Percentage |
| --- | --- |
| Enjoyable | 15 |
| Likeable game | 11 |
| Fun | 6 |
| New/Different | 5 |
| Good at it | 5 |
| Interesting sport | 4 |
| Fitness | 4 |
| Teacher made it interesting | 3 |
| Laugh | 2 |

**Table 1: Top ten reasons for particularly enjoying a sport in PE lessons**

Of course, some of the specific activities on offer were also disliked, but in fact 40% of the pupils claimed not to have disliked any of the sports in PE lessons, and that I think is a remarkably high figure. Do you think many other school subjects match that? I suspect probably not. What is significant is that the sports most commonly disliked, shown in the Table below, were the games and activities more usually on offer in what we could call a 'traditional' PE programme. Seven of the ten – those marked with an asterisk – fall into this category and an eighth, the common substitute that we've probably all experienced on a wet day – cross country running – was popularly hated. Thirty percent of all the pupils who disliked an activity mentioned it.

|  | Rank Order | Number of Pupils |
| --- | --- | --- |
| 1 | Cross-country | 170 |
| *2 | Hockey | 106 |
| *3 | Gymnastics | 85 |
| *4 | Rugby | 82 |
| 5 | Dance | 72 |
| *6 | Athletics | 70 |
| *7 | Swimming | 64 |
| *8 | Cricket | 48 |
| 9 | Jogging | 37 |
| *10 | Netball | 33 |

**Table 2: Top ten activities particularly disliked**

Generally speaking, the PE experience in schools today appears to be pretty popular, and it's as popular with young women as with young men. We were able to compare two single-sex schools in Coventry with identical pupil catchments, often attracting brothers and sisters. The schools had similar social and geographical opportunities, and in each case, well developed PE programmes. The results were remarkable. At Woodlands, the boys school, 89% had found at least one sport that they had enjoyed during their PE career. Tile Hill Wood, the girls school, far from lagging behind, recorded 93%. Obviously the sports on offer at each school are different, but where the same activities were offered, the results were again remarkably similar, as the table below confirms:

| | Woodlands | Tile Hill Wood |
|---|---|---|
| Badminton | 33 | 34 |
| Tennis | 28 | 30 |
| Soccer | 22 | 33 |
| Trampolining | 26 | 19 |
| Rounders/Softball | 20 | 20 |
| Basketball | 15 | 24 |
| Hockey | 15 | 16 |
| Keep Fit/Weight Training | 15 | 13 |
| Swimming | 10 | 21 |
| Athletics | 8 | 9 |

**Table 3: Percentage of players enjoying each activity**

This is not something that is somehow peculiar to Coventry. A quote from a report on a recent study of nearly 1,000 black and ethnic minority young people in Greater Manchester perhaps sums up the position better than I could ever do; it comes from a non-PE specialist, so it isn't looking through rose-tinted glasses:

> *We would emphasise that our over-riding impression from listening to the interviews was the enjoyment evident in the interviewees' voices when they recalled the games and other activities they took part in at school. This enjoyment was equally present both for those who had kept up their participation since leaving school and for those who had not.*

So do most 14-18 year olds really give up sport when outside of their PE lessons? Emphatically no. The General Household Survey, for example, points to a massive involvement amongst 16-19 year olds. Table 4 shows participation over a four week period and the most popular activities are clear. But the bottom line is the most important. Even when walking is excluded, 91% of men and 69% of women take part. This evidence is confirmed by our own surveys in Coventry. We found 73% of 16-18 year olds wanting to continue an existing sport when they left school. In addition, 37% wanted to take up a new sport regularly and 64% wanted to have a go at a new activity.

The important question is, were their aspirations realised? Our follow-up survey three years later shows a high level of participation; 78% were active at the time of the survey and 54% were playing once a week.

Once again the myth that young women find sport irrelevant is dispelled. In fact, more young women had taken up a new sport and more had tried a new sport. However, more men play regularly, but the detailed analysis shows a great deal of flexibility.

It is true that nearly half of all sporting interests had been given up between the ages of 16 and 20, and it is this that accounts for the massive post-school drop out experienced by individual sports. For some sports the statistics make depressing reading:

|  | Proportion of former players dropping out (%) |
|---|---|
| Tennis | 85 |
| Netball | 81 |
| Squash | 80 |
| Hockey | 77 |
| Badminton | 72 |
| Basketball | 66 |
| Rugby | 53 |
| Running/Jogging | 52 |
| Weight training | 50 |
| Cricket | 43 |
| Soccer | 42 |
| Keep fit | 36 |
| Swimming | 32 |

**Table 4: Post-school drop out**

|                                        | Women | Men |
|----------------------------------------|-------|-----|
| Walking                                | 41    | 44  |
| Snooker/Billiards/Pool                 | 23    | 62  |
| Swimming – outdoor                     | 24    | 24  |
| Swimming – indoor                      | 24    | 24  |
| Darts                                  | 11    | 33  |
|                                        |       |     |
| Keep fit/Yoga                          | 24    | 5   |
| Cycling                                | 14    | 28  |
| Athletics – track & field              | 2     | 4   |
| Other running (including Jogging)      | 10    | 18  |
| Football                               | 2     | 40  |
|                                        |       |     |
| Weightlifting/Weight training          | 9     | 22  |
| Golf                                   | 1     | 9   |
| Badminton                              | 12    | 11  |
| Squash                                 | 4     | 8   |
| Table tennis                           | 6     | 14  |
|                                        |       |     |
| Fishing                                | 1     | 7   |
| Tennis                                 | 4     | 6   |
| Tenpin bowls/Skittles                  | 4     | 4   |
| Lawn/Carpet bowls                      | 1     | 2   |
| Cricket                                | 0     | 7   |
|                                        |       |     |
| Water sports (excluding Sailing)       | 2     | 4   |
| Horse riding                           | 6     | 1   |
| Self defence (excluding Boxing)        | 1     | 5   |
| Ice skating                            | 5     | 4   |
| Basketball                             | 1     | 7   |
| Sailing yachts/Dinghies                | 1     | 1   |
|                                        |       |     |
| At least 1 activity (ex. walking) *    | 69    | 91  |
| At least 1 activity *                  | 78    | 93  |
| Base = 100%                            | 678   | 706 |

**Table 5: Percentage participating in the four weeks before interview
(Persons aged 16-19, Great Britain 1987)**

But this is a realignment of interest. It is a drop-off, not a drop-out, at the individual level. **Sport as a whole is still in demand.**

Now we'll move on to the fourth part of the scenario: the notion that young people need to know more about the sports on offer. Remember the Sports Council's lightbulb campaign *Ever Thought of Sport?* In all honesty, our survey evidence shows that young people are now very sports literate and probably don't need to know about what is available. They already know about a whole range of activities through the expanded PE programme and the new links between school and community; Key Stage 3 of the National Curriculum ought to reinforce this.

The barrier is not one of basic knowledge. It is not a campaign or promotional issue, but a practical one of knowing how to get involved. It applies equally to participation and performance sport and I'll return to this later.

So the answer to the next question of whether people need to know where they can play and how to join a club is clear. It is a desperate need.

Some of the most disappointing results from our surveys are the low success rates of people who had a definite aspiration.

---

### All Schools

- 211 out of 295 **continued** existing sport = 71.5%.
- 48 out of 157 **took up** a new sport = 30.5%.
- 19 out of 236 **tried** a new sport = 8%.

*But*

- 22 out of 85 **continued an unintended sport** = 26%.
- 139 out of 380 **took up an unintended sport** = 26%.

---

Those wishing to continue did well, but the level of take-up is disappointing and the fact that only 8% had managed to try a new sport is, in my view, a complete failure on the part of the sporting structure to adapt to young people's aspirations.

However, set against this is the flexibility I referred to earlier; young people who had changed their minds about their involvement. As the panel above shows, a quarter had taken up a sport that they had not mentioned previously. An indication, I believe, of the sports literacy of the current generation.

This literacy is at the level of participation and performance. Young people need to know where they can play casually and how to join clubs. They also need to know where to go to get better at their sports if they are playing regularly. We have also found that it applies to the so-called 'drop-outs' as well. A little bit of positive action and they will take part again. Our survey itself had this effect on one 19 year old:

> *I seem to spend all my spare time with my girlfriend, but now, after seeing everything I've given up on paper, I'm going to make the effort to get back into everything I've dropped. Thanks for making me see what I've been missing.*

Before we move on, let's summarise the situation. Today's young people are generally positive about casual sports, but on their own terms. In general, they know about the options and the range of activities on offer.

True 'drop-outs' are rare. Injuries, social circumstances and disposable income all influence things, but many inactive youngsters are waiting for the chance to take part again when their circumstances change. More importantly, performance opportunities are in demand. Champion Coaching is proving this with the 11-14s, but the over 14s are no different. Many of them are desperate for the chance to get better.

## Involvement on their Own Terms

Let's move on, and address these issues. How do the 14-18 age group get involved in sport on a casual basis, and how do we keep them involved? The reality is that it certainly isn't by promotional campaigns, or even through school or PE teachers.

|  | Percentage |
|---|---|
| Friends | 50 |
| Parents | 18 |
| Own initiative | 14 |
| Relatives | 7 |
| School/Teacher | 7 |
| Other | 4 |

**Table 6: Routes into participation – casual sports**

The parental role is vital, for both young men and young women.

|  | Males % | Females % |
|---|---|---|
| Bought equipment | 53 | 40 |
| Played with pupils | 36 | 26 |
| Paid to play | 42 | 46 |
| Enrolled | 24 | 29 |
| Transported | 38 | 41 |
| Other | 12 | 12 |
| All encouragements | 72 | 72 |

**Table 7: The role of parents – encouragement**

Any of you that have, or have had, fourteen year olds will know that parents are out. Teachers of Years 9 and 10 will tell you that parents are seldom welcomed by their sports team members and for many young women, mothers and fathers may be actively discouraged from showing any interest in their daughters' sporting interests.

Keeping this age group involved is all about treating them as young adults; in school, in the community and in sports clubs. But how do we achieve this?

Firstly, we need to develop their social and interpersonal skills. We need to give them confidence and involve them in planning sport programmes, in managing resources, in future development decisions and in review. As is often the case, there are no young people here this weekend as we review how to address their needs.

Secondly, we need to give them support and training and we need to support the coaches and PE teachers who deliver that training.

---

**Support and Training**

- Identification of talent.
- Support for coaches.
- Support for performance development programmes.
- Support for top level performers.

---

Thirdly, we need to get away from the teacher-led process. This view of after-school sport is typical:

---

**We – the Teachers – Did it all Ourselves**

- Booking facilities.
- Arranging transport.
- Collecting kit.
- Organising equipment.
- Confirming everything.

All the pupils had to do was turn up with little knowledge of the actual organisation of the activities.

---

This means we have to ensure that **education for leisure** is an important part of the way we treat young people. The example in the next panel is typical.

---

**Ice Skating Experience**

- How to find out:
    - Where to skate?
    - How to get there?
    - What sort of clothing?
    - What equipment?
    - When available?
- To know about:
    - How to wear equipment
    - Etiquette / rules
    - Safety requirements.
- And what it is likely to cost
- All **before** how to skate.

---

In addition, we need to ensure that PE and sport in school has a higher profile with partners in the community; with sports clubs; with facility providers; with local community groups; and with the local sports development profession. We also need to ensure that PE as a subject has the resources to offer education for leisure in school.

---

**Higher PE Profile**

- Supportive senior management.
- More responsive staff.
- More flexible support staff.
- PE (or its facilities) making money.
- PE staff more integrated.
- With school governors.

---

Another important aspect is to ensure that we encourage young people to take responsibility for their own leisure, and giving them **leadership skills** is vital. We must develop and support the CCPR's Community Sports Leadership Award programme and make better use of the award holders. Finally, we must ensure that we have co-ordinated opportunities outside school. For example, Youth Sports Action Groups, Teenage Forums and School Sports Committees. We have to listen to the young people. I'll return to this later, but as the following quote shows, young people are quite enlightened these days:

*Sports leaders emphasising group belonging and using outreach into the community can be effective – as you probably know.*

Yes, we know. But are we all committed to helping the sports development profession as local authority cutbacks take their toll? I hope we are. Our 14 year olds deserve our support, but one further message – **adults don't always know best.**

## The Performance Bound Youngsters

Moving on to the performance-bound youngsters, the first question is 'why the concentration on them?' Quite simply, the biggest gap in the sports development continuum of foundation – participation-performance-excellence – is the transition from participation into performance. All the evidence says that traditional sports clubs are not the answer to this gap, but why not?

Some of the young people's comments are revealing. For those who have tried to set up their own clubs, it is the very **club structure** they are trying to emulate that is the problem. As one young lad put it, 'I never expected the catalogue of opposition that we faced whenever we tried to do anything'.

For some young people it is the **overall sporting structure** in which some sports operate:

> *Tennis, squash and badminton are the sports I would like to play.*
> *For the sports named you need a partner to play with or against.*
> *What can you do if none of your friends want to play?*

Perhaps join a club? Well, for many people, the **attitude of clubs** remains a barrier:

> *The only sport that I am interested in is football, both playing and watching.*
> *I am surprised at the reluctance of local teams to take on new players.*

What we have to do, in my view, is to change these attitudes. We need to encourage our clubs to be more outward looking, and to have what has been described as a 'greater community maturity'. We have to start with the National Governing Bodies and with our NGB coaches. I believe NGBs must start to address a range of questions for **each** activity

- Can NGBs respond to the needs of young people outside school?
- Is there a performance structure for those who want to progress?
- Is there a participation structure to complement it?
- Are the best instructors willing and able to work with young people?
- Are the clubs ready to respond – or able?
- Will clubs be willing to work together?
- Who will service and co-ordinate the local framework?

Champion Coaching or similar local initiatives have to be given widespread recognition as the best way to co-ordinate performance sport for the 14 year olds. They do add a new dimension to after-school sport in the following ways:

- Quality guarantee.
- 'Child friendly' exit routes.
- Club/coach contacts on a personal basis.
- Greater parental enthusiasm.
- Partnership 'without any effort'.

Helping to support this effortless partnership is why coach education is so vital. In my view, it is how sport is presented to young people that is important. The monitoring of the first phase of Champion Coaching proved the value of the trained coach. The standard of coaching was the top reason given for the children being attracted to Champion Coaching.

|  | Percentage |
|---|---|
| Good coaching/desire to improve | 39 |
| Attracted to specific sport | 37 |
| Fun | 7 |
| Free gifts | 3 |
| Teacher encouraged | 3 |
| Other | 11 |

Table 8: The Champion Coaching kids – attraction

We also know from our evaluation what the kids most enjoyed about Champion Coaching.

|  | Percentage |
|---|---|
| Improved | 52 |
| Enjoyed sport/fun | 43 |
| Made new friends | 22 |
| Coach was good | 14 |
| Other | 10 |
| (Multiple Response) | |

Table 9: The Champion Coaching kids – reason for enjoyment

They got better, they enjoyed their sport, they had fun, they made new friends, and they thought the coach was good.

There is no doubt that keeping the 14-18 year olds involved at the performance level is down to the coach understanding their needs and aspirations. In our research we have looked closely at the process of developing sport for young performers and I believe it hinges on five important factors:

- Pace.
- Context.
- Style.
- Format.
- Atmosphere.

Firstly, the pace of development is vital. Pushing young people too quickly may lose them, but equally, moving them too slowly may lose the momentum of the initial interest. It won't always be easy, but discussing individual needs with players and with their parents, often helps the individual to articulate where they want to go.

Secondly, the context of this development is important. We have summed this up in our sports development research as follows: 'there is a need to develop a sporting structure that enables individuals to choose the right sport and the right performance context for their own lifestyles'. For performance sport this 'match' is vital. The setting, the timing, the squad structure, the facilities and so on.

Three further factors contribute to the equation: style, format and atmosphere. None of us enjoy our sport if the style is wrong, if the coach has the wrong approach, or if the game is too competitive, or too physical, or too slow moving. Getting the right style is critical. The feedback from Champion Coaching shows the importance of a mixture of games, skills coaching and competition over the 10 weeks. The format has to be right for each child. My own teenage experience of football illustrates the point. I had run around in the cold, the wet and wind with 21 other players for years, getting changed in tatty little huts and heading off home for a shower. Then I found this new format and ran around with 9 other players in a warm, dry sports hall, getting changed in a nice clean changing room and having a warm shower and a gossip afterwards in the café. I might otherwise have dropped off the performance ladder. So too may your performance kids if we get the format wrong.

We have found more young people drop out of activities because the atmosphere is wrong than for any other reason. I didn't like the cold changing room; the dirty floor; the cliquiness; the type of dance music; the unfriendly atmosphere. All of these things are down to individual preferences, but if we are aware of the needs of these individuals, we may be able to guide them to a more appropriate atmosphere; or where the pace of development or the style are more appropriate.

Coaches, in general, need to know much, much more about the social interaction of their young squads than when dealing with older children or adults. Many coaches are beginning to recognise this – a refreshing honesty. As one coach put it:

*They are very complicated and need lots of different stimulants that end in positive praise, so I have expanded my 'vocabulary' and lowered my expectations.*

In short, all coaches need to **understand the process** if young people are to be given the individual choice that they are seeking.

---

**Understanding the Process**

- Identifying precise needs.
- Sensitive guidance.
- Local knowledge of opportunities.
- Local contacts.

---

Identifying the young people's needs and giving sensitive guidance are paramount if the exit route system is to work. The coaches are the eyes, ears and smiles behind performance sport and they need to be able to point the kids towards the most appropriate opportunities.

### A Co-ordinated Approach

The *status quo* has failed young people, and we all accept that. The performance structure at present is too fragmented and that is why we need to have the co-ordinated approach. But co-ordination isn't easy, although we can begin to identify who can do what best. In fact, we have superimposed this on to our own sports development model.

Young people move into performance directly from foundation in many cases – the enthusiastic 11 year olds will be typical. There is a two-way exchange from participation into performance and from performance into participation at a higher level. The match between them, as I keep stressing, is vital. Performance and participation are alongside one another in this version – and they must complement one another.

My original brief for today was to look at what 'the school' could do and what 'the community' could do. I have deliberately avoided the distinction. To create the right structures for young people we need to work together.

The local club and its coaches need to offer the coaching, the training and, in some cases, the venue for performance opportunities. The leisure centres or community sports venues – even if it's the youth club or the local village hall – need to provide the complementary participation opportunities.

The primary school teacher, together with pupils' parents, will have given youngsters the foundation. The PE teachers and youth leaders need to encourage the young players, both into performance sport and into participation by a positive leisure education experience at Key Stages 3 and 4 of the National Curriculum.

Community sports development officers need to be involved in introducing young players to new opportunities outside the education system, and sports specific development officers need to provide the pathways for performance for each sport if the performance bound youngsters are to progress.

At the top, the best coaches must take onboard the top young performers and guide them, helped, where appropriate, by expert sport scientists, sports injuries specialists and sport psychologists.

The vital new addition is in the middle. The Youth Sport Manager or Local Co-ordinator, whose primary role is to bring the interested parties together and to assess where the local community is at – the community audit.

**Community Audit**

- In schools:
    - Equipment.
    - Transport.
    - Special clothing.
    - On-site training facilities.
    - Teacher instructors.
- In the community:
    - Local authority facilities.
    - Outdoor adventure venues.
    - Outdoor sports venues.
- In sporting organisations:
    - Equipment.
    - Instructors.
    - Facilities.
    - Junior sections.
    - Transport.

My final message to you all is to think where you can best contribute to keeping young people involved. I'll finish with my own view of the way forward:

**The Way Forward**

- Community audit.
- Partnership structures.
- Our structures.
- Equality issues.
- Young people's needs.
- Linked opportunities.
- Agreed framework.

A community audit; true partnership structures in place; a recognition of what we can improve about our structures – clubs, NGBs, Sports Council, NCF, BISC, even Government – and how we can take on board equality issues. We need to recognise young people's needs in the 1990s; ensure we have linked opportunities and the community maturity in our clubs and, finally, all contribute to that agreed framework. Most importantly, we must involve the young people themselves in that framework.

Think about it. As coaches, teachers, development officers, or whoever, you all have a role to play **with** young people, not **for** them.

# Playing Together

## Philip Veasey

*Philip Veasey is Assistant Director of the British Schools Lawn Tennis Association. He is currently working on the production of the new LTA Trust Badge Award Scheme and material for the teaching of tennis at Key Stages 3 and 4 of the National Curriculum. Philip is a Panel Tutor for the LTA Tennis Course for teachers, and travels nationwide to deliver this course. He also coaches the National Deaf Tennis Team.*

**Summary of Presentation**

The introduction included:

- common perceptions of tennis
- what was available from the Governing Body
- the important role of the tennis club and the teacher – key players in keeping young people in the game
- case studies of good practice.

The aims and objectives of the British Schools Lawn Tennis Association are to promote and encourage the teaching and playing of tennis in schools, using the following methods:

- Competitions.
- Resources/courses.
- National plan for in-service training.
- National schools tennis coaching programme.
- County schools association.
- Badge award scheme/starter tournaments.
- Clinics/Wimbledon tickets etc..
- Grants for schools courts.
- Coaching courses for students.
- Schools bulletin.

After school opportunities include:

- the Star Club programme
- Champion Coaching
- Short Tennis
- ITI programme
- local authority initiatives
- club development programmes.

There are now 2,000 member schools, with 20,000 pupils playing in the various Midland Bank events. Plans being implemented at present include:

- the placement of coaches in schools to work with the teacher
- provision of a national structure of in-service training for teachers at all key stages of the national curriculum
- the provision of resources for teachers
- ensuring regular communication between the governing body and the teacher
- the introduction of local county schools associations.

# Planning for Success: 'The Best Laid Plans of Mice and Men'

## David Whitaker OBE

*David Whitaker spent fourteen years in the teaching profession, which ran parallel with his sporting career in hockey, as both player and coach. As a player he made over 100 international appearances, and coached the Great Britain side to the first British Olympic Team Gold Medal in over sixty years at the 1988 Olympics. He was Coach of the Year in England in 1985, and UK Coach of the Year in 1985 and 1988. He is a Director of a company which believes that business people can really benefit from his wealth of knowledge and experience through Performance Coaching.*

### Introduction

This is a daunting topic for me because many of you are so skilled in the art of planning for success that I run the risk of covering ground that is well trodden by you already.

With this in mind, I have taken the liberty of coming at this topic from a slightly different perspective and sub-titled it 'The best laid plans of mice and men...'.

I would like us to challenge ourselves in this area of planning: is it enough to have meticulous planning in the obvious areas? I would also like to offer you a framework from my experience of the important elements in developing/promoting high quality performance in individuals and teams, and relate them to our young performers. This is not to devalue our normal areas of planning – it is an essential ingredient – merely to recognise that there are other equally important aspects in achieving successful performance which also need planning. And you will have other ingredients which I do not cover.

You are probably aware of the Japanese word *Kaisen* which means 'in every way getting better and better'. *Kaisen* is for me one of the foundations of my coaching philosophy because it sums up both what I am striving to promote in performers and how I wish to live my life.

So what is success? This is a fundamental question for you in your situation. I do know that success does not have to depend on winning, particularly with young performers, but there has to be a balance between winning vs education for future success. Coaches are in the leadership business – our role is to give direction and purpose to progress. We do not have to be 'the leader' all the while; in fact I believe that is positively dangerous, because during the performance the performers must take responsibility and also, of course, at many other times!

Within this leadership role we must, if we are to perform it well, 'know where we are going'. This may be obvious yet many coaches only 'go where they know'. A slight change in words yet a massive change in 'direction, purpose and progress'. Going where you know is the safe option, whereas knowing where you are going includes the breaking of boundaries and frontiers – a key process in successful performance. Our young performers of tomorrow will need to go beyond where we are today. Do we know where we're going with our young achievers?

In order to lead we plan, and our plans revolve around a whole range of things including:

- Physiological     Playing Programme.
- Psychological     Selection.
- Technical          Financial Aid.
- Tactical            Diet,
                      Lifestyle Management.

I have been along these paths, just as you have, and learnt many things during the journey that enable me to make better and better plans, because we know 'Preparation Promotes Performance', eg:

- Strategic Planning.
- Physiological Planning.
- Lifestyle (Training) Planning.

These three elements are needed to give structure, form, progression and flexibility. They (and others) are important and if these elements are missing they inhibit the opportunity to truly succeed. But do they guarantee success? Well, it depends on your definition of success, but my experience is that they do not because all the top teams have them in abundance in roughly equal measures and the right proportions.

So what are the differences? I would like to offer my insights into the differences on three levels (inextricably inter-connected):

- Personal – within the person.
- Inter-personal – within the interaction of coach and performer.
- Team – within the team.

I believe that there is another level of planning we have to study carefully – the planning of our interaction with our performers. This is a different kind of planning for a dynamic situation.

### Personal
What are the differences at the personal level? We spend much time and planning on technique/tactics/strategies/fitness and yet we have underplanned on the Attitude of Mind – a key part in high quality performance.

My experience is that performers who achieve high levels illustrate Awareness and Responsibility. When we are working with young performers with the objective of achieving high performance, it is important to generate Awareness and Responsibility as this enables them to become decision makers and take greater responsibility for their own development.

I am continually surprised and delighted by the levels of Awareness and Responsibility which young performers can achieve and accept.

How much are we doing in our coaching and what could we do to increase it with the appropriate people?

### Inter-personal

Raising Awareness and Responsibility is a function of how we interact with our performers. We have choices in how we communicate and all of these choices are needed – the skill is in using them appropriately. However, if we want to really generate A and R, then the style of interaction tends to be towards the empowering end. Only **telling** someone to be more responsible can have its difficulties.

If we want performers to become truly A and R then we need to involve them in the learning process – in fact, put them at the centre of it. I found that 'asking' rather than 'telling' promoted this and generated A and R.

The way we interact truly affects our performers' motivation and it is vital that we recognise their needs, not ours. Say what they need to hear to help raise A and R, and not just what you want to say.

If we interact well, then performers can take real responsibility for development without making the coach redundant. What can we do with our young performers to promote this?

### Team

The third area is the growth of the team – the model I use is very simple and focuses on what's going on between people as the team develops organically.

**Co-operation and interdependence.** Let's think of a high performing team – what qualities does it exhibit?

- Supportiveness.
- Leadership.
- Very capable.
- Complementary skills.
- Desire to do better.
- Decisiveness.
- Self healing.
- Focused.
- Trust.
- Mutual respect.
- Flexibility.
- Honesty.
- Empathy.
- Self-belief.
- Common goals.

These qualities and many others enable the team members to perform at a high level, but only with constant attention to process the way they behave with each other.

We want our young performers to take responsibility for helping the team to be successful, and by being supportive and promoting their interaction we can also share in this responsibility.

**Inclusion and dependence.** When performers first join a team, they often feel (and show) their anxiety. They wonder if they are going to fit in, if they will be liked, and if they are good enough. They may feel they have to make an impression, but they don't know the rules.

In order to feel part of the team they will have to depend on the other members to include them, to make them welcome and to make them feel valued. Do we do enough to encourage this feeling of inclusion?

**Assertion and independence.** Performers need to establish their own identity and position within the team so that they have a clear role. Learning to build relationships can develop understanding, and potential conflict within the team can be reduced by bringing issues into the open. Sub-groups may develop, but these can be good for the team in special situations.

I've mentioned some positive aspects, but negative influences are also possible. For example, a closely knit sub-group could become a powerful clique which excluded some team members and ultimately spoiled relationships.

## Conclusion

The whole purpose of planning is to enable performers to achieve the agreed goals (hopefully agreed with performers), and yet many of our written plans are put into action by communication with our performers – and this area also needs to be **planned** – not in quite the same way, but continually monitored by ourselves so that we interact in the way which best promotes performance improvement.

We owe it to our performers to plan the way we interact with them and promote their interaction with one another, so that we truly touch upon the greatest motivation of all – intrinsic motivation.

I wish you well with all your planning.

# Who Needs Parents Anyway?

## Deiniol Williams

*Deiniol Williams is Coordinator of the Sport and Young People Project for the City of Bradford Metropolitan Council. He believes that coaches are the most important element in attracting, encouraging and keeping young people in sports, and works hard towards facilitating their training needs and servicing their coaching requirements. He is currently undertaking an MSc course in 'The Sociology of Sport and Sport Management' at Leicester University.*

Thank you for giving me the opportunity to share with you a few thoughts about an issue which I'm certain most of us here today have thought about at one time or another in our coaching courses, but probably never reached what could be described as a full or complete answer.

While preparing for today I became acutely aware that the answer is both simple and complicated. Simple, in the sense that we all need parents whether we are children, adults, teachers, policemen, coaches, Ministers of the Crown, or members of the Royal Family. In terms of sport, however, the answer is slightly more complicated, and perhaps we can share a few ideas about this.

Perhaps I can begin by explaining how I have arrived where I am today in a sporting and development sense.

For the past three years I have been working on a project called Sport and Young People – loosely based on Coventry's Active Life Styles – and partly funded and supported by the Yorkshire and Humberside Sports Council. The project has examined ways of creating a structure in Bradford which will attract young people into sport, and even more importantly, help them to stay in sport. Although the project has an 8-18 age span remit, we have tended to concentrate on children and young people from age nine upwards, ie. middle and upper school pupils.

However, between 1980 and 1990, I worked on Bradford's Swimming Development Plan which incorporated a wide number of aquatic activities, including a very successful Learn to Swim Scheme. It was the experience I gained while working on this scheme that has helped me to formulate many of the ideas that I shall be discussing. I should add that many of the suggestions that I will make this afternoon were not necessarily carried out; some were, but obviously more were not. I have arrived at these ideas today by looking back and saying, 'I wish I'd done that when I had the chance'; and also, long after the event, it's a case of saying, 'what did I learn from that?'.

Next, I would like to have a look at the path that Sports Development and Coaching has taken. Over the past twenty or so years we have seen the following:

- An emphasis on people (children and adults) participating – taking part in sporting activities largely through the influence of campaigns, foster days, courses, Award schemes, and so on. Some have been successful, others have failed.

- NGBs have trained their coaches so that they are expert in teaching/coaching sports, particularly in a technical competency sense.

- Facility and resource design and provision of swimming pools, sports centres, athletics arenas, etc. in both the public and the private sector.

- As a consequence, facility management became a science in itself, with the emphasis on providing good customer care, with clean, smart premises and well constructed programmes taking over from the previous 'take it or leave it' formula. Sporting facilities became marketable facilities and Local Authorities and managers took up the challenge of CCT.

- The understanding and appreciation of adequate funding being one of the keys to a successful sports programme. Sponsorship and other forms of external funding schemes became available and much sought after.

These have all been the development of physical factors – taking part and place in a haphazard and sometimes chaotic manner, but nevertheless creating other, slightly more philosophical and less tangible factors. Things like the development of the Sports Development Continuum with its recognition of the four major components – Foundation, Participation, Performance and Excellence. This has helped many of us to locate ourselves in sport and helped us not only to identify where our contribution to sport lies, but also where it can lead to.

The 'catch 'em young' philosophy has also emerged. Only the other day I heard someone say, possibly correctly, that if a youngster hasn't made it in gymnastics by the age of fourteen she might as well forget it. Come back Vera Czaslavska – all is forgiven.

All these factors have helped Sports Development and Coaching to emerge as recognisable disciplines within the world of sport.

This is the scenario within which I operate as the Sports Development Officer, paying particular attention to the provision of sporting opportunities to young people. To me, these are the essential ingredients in this wonderful cake-mix we know as sports development.

So, now we shall go back to the original question – let's see if we can arrive at some sort of an answer, and also, if we can ask some other questions of ourselves which might clarify the answer even further.

During the preparation of this paper I became increasingly curious about how parents and their roles were perceived by those who were given the tremendous responsibility of writing reports and recommendations about young people and sport. My curiosity was fuelled by my own experience, firstly as a parent (a member of the rising army of people who have ruined many a car by transporting whole teams and substitutes to matches) and secondly, as someone who has 'used' (hopefully not abused) parents in the pursuance of several of my previous posts as PE teacher and Sports Development Officer.

When I started looking at how parents were 'officially' recognised, what I found made pretty dismal reading.

During my preparation, I took the opportunity to re-read several documents on Sport and Young People; a few of them are listed below:

- *Sport and Young People – Partnership and Action* (The School Sports Forum 1989)

  Only two of the 69 recommendations mention **parents,** and the emphasis here is very much on the 'Parents should...' syndrome.

- *School-Aged Sports in Scotland* (The Scottish Sports Council – 1989)

  There is a brief reference to 'playing sport with other members of the family' (parents, not specified). There are no recommendations regarding **parents** anywhere in the report apart from a passing reference to them as 'part of the human resources' that could be used.

- *Young People and Sport, The Sports Council's Consultation Document* (Midlands 1992)

  Parents are mentioned twice in Sub-Objective 1.1 in relation to providing play activity; and in Sub-Objective 2.1 where reference is made towards providing a joint education/training package for parents, guardians and teachers etc. Unfortunately, in the recently produced response to this document, no mention of parents can be found at all.

- *A Regional Strategy Topic Study on Sport and Young People* (West Midlands Sports Council 1988)

  Again, no mention of parents, although to be fair the study does contain a résumé of Coventry's Active Life Styles Project which itself studied parents' contribution in introducing youngsters to sport.

However, there's good news as well as bad news...

First of all, the collection of papers presented at the 1989 BISC conference contains an interesting paper by Steve Rowley, based on the TOYA study and examines the effect of the intensive training on family life.

- *The Independent Assessment of the Champion Coaching Project (1992)* gives a clear indication that parents' comments can and should be listened to, because they have something to say too.

- Finally, although very small in comparison with its heftier companions, the NCF's Introductory Study Pack 7 *Working with Children* makes several references to the relationship that coaches should have with parents, who are described as 'influential people' and 'significant others'. This is a definite step in the right direction.

- Even in the above examples, references to parents are in the context of either 'older' children, ie. 15-16 or elite performers. Even the report on the Champion Coaching Project deals with children in the participation/performance bands.

There is, therefore, virtually no official recognition of parents' contribution and role, particularly in relation to the foundation stage – which is what we should confine ourselves to today.

Secondly, I was interested in who the people were that made up the group charged with the responsibility of producing the reports referred to previously. I suppose that many of them were parents, but I wonder how many of them, and to what extent, and in what way, allowed their feelings as sporting parents to influence their opinions and hence their recommendations. They appear not as parents, but as people holding down posts having achieved some sporting level of excellence.

By now I hope you can begin to see that what I'm looking for is recognition of the value of parents' contribution and work in children's sporting experience.

Next, I would like to ask you a few questions, not so much that you can provide me with answers, but they are questions that you can perhaps ask yourselves.

### Q1 – To what extent do you recognise parents?
To help you arrive at an answer, let me give you two examples. Some years ago, I was interviewing a group of swimming coaches for a full time coaching position in Bradford, and one of them had some experience of coaching swimming in America. He told me of one coach who operated at an outdoor pool separated from a large car park by the changing accommodation. There were two entrances to the building with 'Swimmers' and 'Parents' clearly written above the two. The entrance with Swimmers led to a passage way which in turn led to the changing rooms and then to the pool. The one with Parents led to a long, unlit passage way which led directly back to the car park!

Let's call that the American Experience. Although I recognise that it may well have been an isolated incident, it is nevertheless an example of a prevalent attitude among many coaches.

The other example is one I call the Bradford Experience. This is one where the coach (again in swimming) makes every effort humanly possible to make the parents' morning and evening next to the pool a pleasant one – easy chairs, TV, Tea/Coffee facility, canned music etc. They enjoy the experience, even at 5.30am in the morning.

### Q2 – Which of the two examples is nearest to your own experience?
If you're a long way off both, and would like to get to one or the other refer to the next question.

### Q3 – What would you have to do, or go through to arrive?

### Q4 – What do you think the reaction of the parents would be, and how would you cope with that reaction?

The answers to all these questions, I leave to you. Nevertheless, I think they are interesting questions to ask because the answers may well give you an indication of your recognition of parents' real value or worth to your sports programme. So now let's start examining parents' contributions to your programme in particular, and to sports in general.

As 'sports professionals' we are often referred to as 'the deliverers', but we may well find that we fulfil a fairly minor role when we compare our role, our contribution, with that of parents.

For example:

- Parents are people.
- Parents are coaches (coaches are parents).
- Parents (help) run clubs.
- Parents represent funding – annual membership, weekly fees, equipment, travel, etc.
- Parents pay for facilities through Income Tax and Council Tax.

Most importantly, parents provide the moral and ethical framework that children need for their journey through life, so in other words, parents deliver.

The inevitable question is, do we as Sports professionals deliver the same amount in terms of quantity and quality?

I believe, and I'm certain that you do too, that we all need parents, as they say in Yorkshire 'whether or not'. So, having established the fact that we do need them, have we ever asked what to me is the most important question of all, 'What do parents need?'

Before we come to the conclusion of the paper and conduct an examination of the needs of parents, let me add another important word. That word is **commitment**. Parents deliver commitment by the barrel load. And before I get to some of the more emotive issues surrounding the area of the needs of parents, let me examine one or two ideas which are directed at you, the coaches and sport development officers. These are the ideas that coaching can be concerned not only with the delivery of the sport, but also about delivering committed people – both children and adults, even those who are only just beginning their sporting careers at the foundation level.

I believe that coaching is creating parents (and children) who:

- have a sense of purpose
- can truly contribute
- have security, including full information
- have personal preference (as expressed).

Can I ask that you take these four issues on board, and examine how you, through your methodology, can produce an even more committed group of children and parents. This can only be good for sport. This could be your contribution for the well-being of sport, probably of more value than producing a cup winning team, or a medal winning athlete.

Finally, what have we learnt from the issues that I've raised?

Without a doubt, sport needs parents. So, if that need is there, then you as coaches and Sports Development Officers need to address the issue of how you can develop the environment in which parents as well as children can flourish, and by doing so, enhance your organisation and your sport.

Let me leave you with the following ideas regarding parents' needs:

- Recognise and appreciate – say thanks to them, often.
- Love them for what they do and for being what they are.
- Encourage them to fulfil their potential within your organisation in particular, and within sport in general.
- Make sure that you create the environment that will allow them to have their voices heard.
- Give, or offer them counselling, particularly when things go wrong.

In conclusion, it would be remiss of me to think or suggest that you do not do these things, or that you do not give recognition to parents' contribution to sport. However, my point is that every coach should have a personal policy of doing these things and actually have a plan to action them on a regular basis – and mean it. Daft as it may seem, a 'parent of the month' award would be even more appreciated than 'player of the month' or 'most valuable player of the match'. Create some little gimmick to award deserving parents on a regular basis.

Make this the first step in recognising the true value and worth you place on your sporting parents.